# For Pastors
### of small churches

## By Kent Philpott

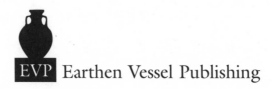 Earthen Vessel Publishing

# Earthen Vessel Publishing

289 Miller Avenue
Mill Valley, California 94941

415-381-3061 Email: kentphilpott@home.com
Web: www.earthenvessel.net
Miller Avenue Baptist Church web: www.w3church.org

---

Publisher and senior editor: Kent Philpott
Layout and graphic design: Margaret J. Bates
Editor: Dawn LaRue
Distribution: Lisa Philpott
Marketing: Grace Reed
Web Master: Bill Reed

Laura and Jenna Philpott's pottery work provided the inspiration for both the cover and the name of our publishing company.

First published 2000

ISBN    0-9703296-0-1

---

Printed and bound in the Untied States.

But we have this treasure in earthen vessels,
so that the surpassing greatness of the power
will be of God and not from ourselves.

2 Corinthians 4:7 (New American Standard)

# Contents

# Table of Contents

# Foreword

I have served as pastor of a small church for over twenty-one years. My congregation is still among those churches with an active membership barely above one hundred. If you are a pastor of a church with less than 150 active and tithing members, this book will teach you more than you will ever learn in a traditional seminary.

I earned three Masters degrees and one Doctorate from a well-known and fully accredited seminary. I was well schooled in the principles of Biblical interpretation; I learned Greek and Hebrew from some of the best teachers. I studied church history and systematic theology. The one thing I was not prepared for was ministry in a small church. Since most churches are small churches, you would think that the average seminary would do a good job preparing its students for ministry in the small congregation. However, many theological institutions will not prepare you for what you will face in a small church.

This book will do more for the average pastor of a small congregation than years of training in a traditional school. The book is very practical. Kent should have written this book twenty years ago. It would have saved me countless sleepless nights. Some of the ideas are radical but solidly biblical and theologically sound. The most important thing about this book is that it is very practical. It is written in the format of "books for dummies." The wisdom shared by Philpott is priceless.

The book is full of practical ideas gained by the author's own experience as pastor of a small church. Of all the books I have read on the small church, this is the only book written specifically for the pastor of a small congregation. Whether you are seminary trained or not, I highly recommend this book as a "must" for your personal library.

Emmanuel Akognon
President and Academic Dean
Southern Marin Bible Institute
Marin City, California

# Foreword

If you had lived two thousand years ago and had the privilege to meet Jesus face to face, there are a couple of words I doubt you would use to describe your experience. Regardless of your theological perspective, no matter what your spiritual or emotional state, you would probably never say that Jesus was boring or irrelevant.

Jesus challenged his friends and angered his foes. He inspired, healed and loved the people around him, like no one before or since. Yet many pastors who claim to be followers of Jesus conduct meetings in his name that are often boring and irrelevant. What is worse is that some pastors live their lives without the health and vitality that characterized the life of Jesus. This should not be so.

I went to a friend's wedding a while ago that reminded me why I quit going to church for several years as a teenager. The building was beautiful, but the wedding itself started late and dragged on for an hour. I couldn't wait for it to be over.

Another wedding I attended more recently brought laughter, tears and joy to everyone involved. A religious service has great power to inspire us when it is conducted in a relevant, personal way. The same can be said about the life of a minister. Some Christian leaders live depressed and frustrated lives. They lack the wisdom and power of the Holy Spirit. There is a great need for those who lead God's people to learn the wisdom, which can enable them to be fruitful. This book is filled with Kent Philpott's practical insights that helped me when I first met him almost thirty years ago.

I was a confused twenty-year-old when I met Kent in May of 1970. His living room in San Rafael, California was crowded with young people singing praises and studying the Bible. The "Jesus Movement" was just starting in Northern California and Kent was in the center of it.

Kent had opened up his home for Bible studies and evangelism around the clock. We were drawn together by curiosity, adventure and the Spirit of God. Kent had gone to seminary where he had become grounded in the truth that a whole new generation was hungry to learn. He led meetings with a guitar in his hands and preached in a language we could relate to.

Through relevant Bible teaching and counseling with prayer, Kent helped hundreds of young people enter the Kingdom of God. He steered us away from the cults and talked us through our trials.

As the ministry grew, we started numerous Bible studies, discipleship houses and Christian bookstores. In 1972, we started a church. By 1976 we had four churches. These churches grew and began their own mission outreaches. During those years we went through numerous struggles and trials. We saw leaders rise and fall. We made mistakes and learned many lessons the hard way.

Much of the fruit of those years remains, not in any one church or organization, but in hundreds of people, now middle aged, who are faithfully serving the Lord around the country.

As my pastor and friend, Kent helped me to grow and mature. He gave me training and opportunities, which prepared me for a lifetime of ministry. Kent understands the practical steps pastors and ministers need to take to build a fruitful ministry. His wisdom and counsel in this book will be a treasure for everyone who seeks to influence people the way Jesus did.

Mark Buckley, pastor
Living Streams Christian Church,
Phoenix, Arizona

# Foreword

Through my fifty years plus in the gospel ministry it has been my privilege to see not only hundreds of young men accept the Lord Jesus Christ, but also many of these have entered the gospel ministry. One such man is Kent Philpott. I have had the privilege of watching his ministry throughout the years and can say that God's hand has been richly upon him. The several books that he has authored are outstanding works based upon biblical principles. One such book, *Are You Really Born Again?* should be read by every preacher of the gospel as well as every Christian, because I fear that many have not experienced genuine conversion. And now Kent has written this book for pastors with an emphasis on the small church.

After having read several chapters of the book and examined an annotated table of contents it would be my personal desire that this would be a required reading by all young pastors, both in college or in seminary. Most of it is practical information, things I have encountered in my own pastoral ministry. And though college and seminary were a blessing to me, there was not one thing that I learned in these institutions that actually prepared me to be a pastor of a church. If I had had a book such as Kent has written before I started out it would have saved me a lot of time and effort. For you see, there are many things that you can not any other way than by actually doing the work.

Here Kent encourages keeping the main thing the main thing—that is—focusing on the gospel and evangelism, bringing people to faith in Christ, and helping them grow up into Him, which we call discipleship.

One way we can keep our churches on the right tract, as expressed by one of my college professors, is in this saying: "Young man, remember that an old Arkansas mule can't kick and pull at the same time." I understood that to mean, "If Christians keep doing the main thing they will not have time to fight over non-essentials."

Kent addresses many things that I have learned the hard way in the ministry, such as working in my own community. No one in seminary taught me anything about the opportunities I would have in conducting funerals. And no one taught me anything about counseling and performing marriages. Little did I know that there was more to the pastoral ministry than teaching and preaching never learned the value of working with city agencies and civic organizations. I have had the pleasure of serving in my community in many capacities; it has been a major part of my ministry. I suggested to Kent that he add something about this in his book, but he says that this has not been something he has had experience with. But I would encourage pastors to be involved in and attend local government meetings and get to know the way things work. Attend meetings even when you have no special interest in the proceedings. As a result of my community activities I am well know and have the opportunity to act as pastor to many people who are not involved in any church.

And I recommend that pastors be engaged with their children, for a pastor who loses his children has not really been successful. I think you will find that this is Kent's view as well.

In closing, I find it most gratifying to have been Kent's first pastor and that he received the Lord Jesus Christ in the church I happened to have pastored, the First Baptist Church of Fairfield. Kent is a man who loves the Lord and who loves people, and especially he loves preachers. And he hopes to help preachers learn things that are hard to come by.

May God's blessing be upon all of you who read this book.

Foreword by Robert D. Lewis, pastor,
Temple Baptist Church, (SBC),
Fairfield, California.

# Preface

This book is primarily for pastors of small churches. Friends have told me the book will be useful for pastors of large churches as well. But I had the small church in mind since little is written for the small church and the bulk of my experience is with the small church.

Most churches are small churches and they are and always have been the backbone of Christianity. Someone cautioned me that this was a small target audience. Perhaps, yet I have in mind the thousands of students in Bible colleges, institutes, and seminaries who are preparing for the pastoral ministry. In addition, pastors are usually readers and they are the ones who frequently recommend books to members of their congregations. And if all this were not true, it is pastors who I want to reach out to because they are the most influential group, in terms of the kingdom of God, on the planet.

What are my qualifications for writing this book? I can not say I am a "wise" or "mature" pastor, but I have some experience as a pastor. I pastored a church in my seminary days, from 1966 to 1968, after which I was leader of a para-church ministry for five years, but essentially that was also pastoring, preaching, teaching, and organizing. And then, for eight years, I pastored a church I had an opportunity to co-found. Later on I functioned as an associate (minister at large) for several years before beginning another church, Miller Avenue Baptist Church, where I am now in my sixteenth year. At age 58 I find that I have been in ministry since the early part of 1966. So I have become an experienced, if not a wise and mature, pastor.

Each chapter begins with a true-to-life experience that highlights the significance of that chapter's subject. Questions and statements appear at the conclusion of each chapter designed to provoke thought, discussion, or reflection about that chapter's subject, or they could also be used for discussion in a classroom setting.

This book is a ministry project of Miller Avenue Baptist Church of Mill Valley, California, an American Baptist congregation. It has been my privilege and usually my pleasure to serve as the founding and continuing pastor from July 1, 1985. Ours is a small church, forty on Sunday morning is a crowd, and our focus is preaching the gospel, teaching, service, missions, prayer, and growing up into the fullness of Christ.

An experienced pastor may read this book and say, "I could have written this". And I would agree. I welcome additions, corrections, suggestions, and other points of view. This may be seen as a "work in progress" or "under construction". Therefore, if anyone would like to talk with me about the contents of this book please write to me at 285 Miller Avenue, Mill Valley, CA 94941. If you would like to email me send it to: kentphilpott@home.com., or w3church.org. Or you can visit the web sites: www.earthenvessel.net, or www.w3church.org.

Margaret Jane Bates, a long-time member of Miller Avenue and art director of Earthen Vessel

Publishing, transcribed audiotapes onto which I had recorded the contents of this book. My wife Lisa is working with distribution and general encouragement of the author. My daughter, Dory LaRue, helped edit the manuscript. If you see anything amiss, errors and what not, lay that to may credit. (You might also notify me of errors for correction in future editions.) My daughter, Grace Reed, is helping with marketing. Grace's husband Bill put our website, earthenvessel.net, together. My twin ten year old daughters, Laura and Jenna, will be of help in ways not known right now.

Though this book is copyrighted, anyone, for whatever purpose, may use any or all of the material in the book without obtaining permission from myself or Earthen Vessel Publishing. The material may be copied, distributed, or whatever else.

All Bible quotations, except where noted, are from the New International Version.

Kent Philpott,
Mill Valley, California

# One

# On Preaching the Gospel

One day toward the end of my first year as pastor
of Miller Avenue Baptist Church, a young man knocked
at the door of my office. He had spent the better part
of the day going from one church and pastor to another
asking how he could become a Christian. For months
he had been reading the Bible and listening to
television and radio preachers, and he was determined
to get to the bottom of it.

By the time he got to me he was frustrated and
confused. "Are you going to tell me to join your
church?" he asked with an edge to his voice. "I suppose
you want to baptize me?"

"Sit down a minute, relax, and let me tell you the
gospel," I said as reassuringly as possible. For twenty
minutes or so I told him about the finished work of
Jesus. In the midst of my presentation he suddenly
declared, "Oh, I see now, Jesus did it for me." An hour
later, he left, at peace; the seeker had been found. That
encounter became one of the highlights of my ministry.

✟   ✟   ✟   ✟   ✟

This story dramatically illustrates the centerpiece
of the gospel. This man wanted one thing—the

good news of Jesus and when he heard it he knew it was what he sought.

Of first importance then, let me outline what I believe the gospel is.* Paul, in 1 Corinthians 15:1-5 presents the apostolic gospel:

> Now, brothers, I want to remind you of the gospel I preached to you, which you received and on which you have taken your stand. By this gospel you are saved, if you hold firmly to the word I preached to you. Otherwise, you have believed in vain. For what I received I passed on to you as of first importance: that Christ died for our sins according to the Scriptures, that he was buried, that he was raised on the third day according to the Scriptures, and that he appeared to Peter, and then to the Twelve.

The gospel is Jesus, both who He is and what He did. Christianity is Jesus Christ Himself. To preach the gospel is to preach Jesus. Someone has said that good preaching is bragging about Jesus. Jesus is God in the flesh, at once truly and completely God and truly and completely man. Jesus is the eternal, uncreated Son of the Father, who freely choose to empty Himself, take on flesh, and be born of the Virgin Mary. Having lived a sinless life, He was crucified and died under the administration of the Roman governor Pontius Pilate in about 33AD. He was buried and on the third day He rose bodily from the grave. He ascended to heaven forty days later, where He is now seated at the right hand of the throne of God, which is the place of power and authority. He will come again a second time to judge the living and the dead. He is the Lord of all and ultimately all knees will bow to Him.

Jesus died in our place as our substitute. He took our sin upon Himself. His death satisfied the just demand of a holy and righteous God who is offended by sin. The blood that Jesus shed cleanses those who trust in Him, completely washing away all sin, past, present, and future. Jesus' work on the cross justifies sinners, and at once the sinner is declared righteous. This righteousness is imputed or placed within those who trust and come to Him. By the working of God's Spirit we are able to repent and believe; both repentance and faith are gifts of grace. This is conversion or the new birth, and at that moment the sinner is indwelled by the Holy Spirit and given eternal life. "Justification by faith" is the great, biblical and reformation truth. "Sole fide,"—faith in Jesus alone brings salvation.

This gospel must be faithfully and honestly presented to the unconverted. The gospel preacher is Christ's ambassador, and should speak as though God Himself was making a personal appeal. The gospel preacher beseeches, implores, and pleads for sinners to be reconciled to God. (see 2 Corinthians 5:20) Good preaching incorporates earnest pleading with the unconverted to come to Jesus; an impassioned call to trust in Jesus alone is the singular characteristic of the great preachers. Additionally, the preacher is an ambassador for Christ and not the church, a creed, or a theological system.

The gospel preacher urges trust in Jesus beyond a mere intellectual understanding that Jesus died and rose again; simply accepting facts will not result in new birth. The facts of the gospel are to be preached as well as the need to turn to Jesus in repentance and faith. A person may acknowledge and confess doctrinal truth yet remain unconverted. Conversion is coming to Jesus and trusting that His shed blood is sufficient to atone for sin.

The gospel is heard through the preached Word. (see 1 Corinthians 2:4) As the gospel is preached, the Holy Spirit both convinces of sin and draws or calls a person to Jesus. The preacher is never able, by the use of clever means, to make salvation happen; the preacher must rely upon the Holy Spirit to bring about true conversion.

Is preaching the gospel a pastor's only task? No! It is one of many aspects of pastoral ministry, which is broad and almost limitless. Ministry is service to Jesus and His Church. It is accomplished with varying gifts, service and working. (see 1 Corinthians 12:4-6) When a model of pastoral ministry is sought in the Scripture, one is not easily found. Most concepts of pastoral ministry are rooted in tradition. The pastor visits, counsels, administrates, prays, teaches, preaches, leads worship, and an "etc." must be added.

In my view though, a pastor's chief responsibility is the preaching of the gospel so that unconverted people might come to Jesus.

Most churches are structured so that the pastor bears the bulk of the gospel-preaching responsibility, unless there is a resident evangelist or apostle. According to some New Testament expositors, all "normal" churches would have evangelists and apostles whose primary focus would be preaching the gospel. (see Ephesians 4:11-12) I am not personally aware of churches that have a ministry office designated "apostle" or "prophet" or "evangelist." Most small churches typically have one pastor/teacher, and such is the case at Miller Avenue Baptist Church. Therefore, it falls upon me to be the evangelist. I carry the responsibility of proclaiming the gospel. If there were

4

another pastor serving alongside me, then I would be free to do the work of evangelism. Until then, I am charged with preaching the gospel and leading in the church's ministry.

My great joy is to preach the gospel, whether to a small or large group, or to a single individual. I have often said that when it comes to being a pastor, I don't rate high on the giftedness scale. On a scale of one to ten, I probably am rating a four. But as an evangelist I would probably get a six. I would imagine there are many pastors like me.

The typical congregation is blessed with a wide variety of spiritual gifts. However, few are called to preach the gospel. In Romans 10:14 Paul asks, "How can they believe in the one of whom they have not heard? And how can they hear without someone preaching to them?" In verse 17, Paul then says, "Faith comes from hearing the message, and the message is heard through the word of Christ." Clearly, there is no greater joy than preaching the gospel. It is the highest calling of pastoral ministry, for *How beautiful are the feet of those who bring good news* (Romans 10:15).

I do not believe the gospel message is to be tacked casually or perfunctorily onto the end of a sermon. When preaching a conversion oriented sermon, I will do so from beginning to end. When I preach strictly to the converted, the entire sermon will be of a practical nature. This is generally true, but not always an accurate description of my method. Sometimes I will give the gospel out when preaching to believers. We can never be sure that all whom we think are converted actually are.

In any case, I feel that preaching the gospel is my primary calling in pastoral ministry, and I will do it in whatever way I can. I pursue it on Sunday mornings, and through a community access television program. I regularly send out audiotapes of my sermons to a long list of people. In the past year and a half more than 2300 tapes were mailed. It is not self-promotion, just another way of presenting the gospel.

Preaching the gospel must be emphasized for two main reasons. First, unconverted people do not feel comfortable hearing the gospel because it offends them. When they hear of their need to turn away from sin and trust Jesus, the internal conviction of sin is uncomfortable. Many people think that Christianity is simply about love and that there are many paths to God. When a straightforward gospel message is preached that rejects such popular notions, there will be offense. The object of that offense is often-times the preacher. The preacher will sense this and may be tempted to soften the gospel message or cease from preaching it altogether.

Second, and worst of all, is the offense of the "Christianized", those who suppose they are genuine Christians, but in fact are not. I have a particular sensitivity to them because I have helped to christianize so very many in the course of my ministry. For twenty-nine years I did not understand the mystery of conversion and the tremendous danger of false conversion. The Christianized are not able to tolerate conversion-oriented sermons. A fear they do not understand arises within them and they feel threatened. The Christianized generally prefer positive sermons with inspiring stories. They contend they need something that will motivate, inspire, encourage, and support them. They favor "how to" sermons—how to overcome anger, how to be successful in a crazy world, how to be this or that.

The converted, in contrast, love to hear the gospel preached. Such preaching builds them up and helps them grow up into the fullness of Jesus. "I love to tell the story", "Tell me the old, old story," the words of these great hymns reflect the heart of those who are genuinely born again.

The preaching of the gospel cuts like a double-edged sword—it brings both life and death. Here is Paul's assessment: "For we are to God the aroma of Christ among those who are being saved and those who are perishing. To the one we are the smell of death; to the other, the fragrance of life. And who is equal to such a task (2 Corinthians 2:15-16)?

Pastors preach the gospel, preach it with clarity and strength. For many pastors this is their greatest source of satisfaction. There is no greater joy than to preach the good news of Jesus Christ.

☞ Concerning the young man in the opening vignette, would you have spoken to him differently?

☞ How would you describe the primary purpose of your ministry?

☞ Would you add or subtract anything from my view of the gospel?

*I include a presentation of the basic content of the gospel because I did not know much of it in the early years of my ministry and therefore I do not assume that everyone has a clear grasp of it. Of course, I thought I knew the gospel as a new pastor and would have felt insulted if anyone had suggested I did not. I do find though that my understanding of the gospel seems to grow; I am still learning it.

Two

# The Call to Pastoral Ministry

"I only went into the ministry because my parents wanted me to. I can't take it anymore and now it is too late for me to do anything else."

Desperate words from a desperate man and what a tragedy for him and his family. At age fifty he felt there was no where else to go. "Why didn't someone stop me, why didn't anybody sit me down and talk to me for real?" he wondered.

✧    ✧    ✧    ✧    ✧

Before entering the pastoral ministry it is necessary to be as clear as possible that it is the will of God. And this is not easily known. Though most of us speak as if our call was clear and undeniable, still for many it was not always so. Family and friends may say, after observing certain talents and skills, "You are ideally suited for the ministry." A person may want to be an electrical engineer for instance, but due to some success doing ministry at a local church, people are doing their best to send the young person off to seminary. Any call must come directly to a person and not to family or friends. Success in ministry must not be equated with a call either.

Every Christian is called to ministry—to serve and honor God. We are to be prepared to give the reason for our hope. (1 Peter 3:15) And we are all sent to bear witness to Jesus and the gospel. (John 20:21) Yet I believe there is a distinct call to the pastoral ministry beyond the call and election of every Christian. At the very least, before entering into ministry, a person must be clear about what it means to be a preacher and pastor.

It is difficult to express the actual call to pastoral ministry, and probably impossible to describe what it feels like, if it feels like anything at all. Some people express it in terms of feelings and emotions. This was not true of me personally. Not that I am devoid of emotion, but I am not a terribly excitable person (outside of sports, that is). When it comes to religious things, in fact, I've learned to mistrust my feelings and emotions; I do not equate them with the moving of the Holy Spirit in my life. I have found Scripture more reliable than my feelings. I don't deny my feelings, but they need to be corroborated by Scripture.

Is a "call" biblical? Is it something very specific and obvious? Frankly, both questions are difficult to answer. From Scripture we know that Jesus called the Twelve to Himself. (Mark 1:16-20) They did not chose Him, He chose them. This is the great precedent. Also, Jesus called Paul, specifically and concretely. The seven deacons were also chosen or appointed, especially called out from the congregation. (Acts 6:2-3) Ephesians 4:11 states that God "gave some to be apostles, some to be prophets, some to be evangelists, and some to be pastors and teachers." The word "gave" used in this verse is from the ordinary Greek verb for "to give". It does not convey a meaning of appointment or ordination, just simple "gave". But it is God who initiated the process. This is what I consider "the call".

9

As I suggested in the first paragraph of this chapter, the obviousness of a call is debatable. My own "call" was undeniable, so much so that it is yet fresh in my mind. I simply wanted to be a preacher, nothing else mattered, and a way was opened up for me to pursue my desire. I have read many other descriptions of a call to ministry and I do not dispute any of them. This is far from an exact science.

My favorite description of the call to preach is found in a book by D. Martin Lloyd-Jones' entitled, *Preaching and Preachers* (Zondervan Publishing House, 1971). In the chapter "The Preacher", four points about a call to ministry stand out in my mind. One, there is an inner, a subjective drawing to the ministry. No person puts it there; it is specifically and uniquely yours. Two, there is a burden for unbelievers and an accompanying desire to do something about it. Three, there is a sense of "constraint," that is, you can do nothing else than be a preacher. Lloyd-Jones quotes Spurgeon who said to his students that if you can do anything else, stay out of the ministry. And I very much agree with the great Spurgeon. Four, there should be a sense that the calling is so awesome that it is beyond you, that you are not worthy of it, that you are inadequate for it. It is just as Paul asked, "Who is equal to such a task" (2 Corinthians 2:16)?

Such was the case with my own call to ministry. At the time I was pursuing a masters degree in psychology, at Sacramento State University in Sacramento, California. Right in the middle of a certificate program in counseling (I intended to be a school psychologist) I quit and took off for seminary. I had a growing sense that the only thing that mattered *for me* was to be a preacher of the gospel. I had an overwhelming desire to be in full time ministry in some capacity, either as an evangelist, missionary, or pastor.

At that point in my life I had many interests. I enjoyed playing baseball and surfing. I sought out adventure and great challenges. I even liked being in the military. I enjoyed going to college. But nothing was of truly great interest to me.

I had always been interested in psychology. I spent five years earning a bachelor's degree taking far more psychology courses than I needed. But, when I saw the gospel for what it was, psychology did not interest me as much any more. I couldn't imagine a career as a psychologist; it seemed a trivial pursuit. Psychology was no longer at the center of what I wanted, but gospel ministry was everything to me.

It does not seem to me that I had any other call than that—nothing else interested me. I could have earned my livelihood as a school psychologist and found other avenues of service and ministry. I certainly could have, but that was not in my mind. If it had been suggested that I could be a school psychologist and a preacher of the gospel all at once I might have said, "Yes, that sounds like a good idea to me." But I also wanted the training; I wanted to spend time studying the Bible. I wanted to learn about church history and theology. I already had a desire to learn Greek and Hebrew. I had heard various seminary professors and my own pastor, Robert Lewis at First Baptist Church of Fairfield, (he is now pastor of Temple Baptist Church in Fairfield) talk about Greek words and Hebrew words, and I wanted to know those words. I wanted to be able to handle a Greek New Testament. I wanted to know who Martin Luther and John Calvin were. I had heard the names of great Christian heroes mentioned, but I knew nothing of them. So in my own mind this was my call. Everything else began to fade in importance. The only meaning I could find was in gospel ministry. It wasn't so much that I wanted to be the pastor of a church, I just wanted to preach the gospel.

There was one major moment in 1965 when everything about my call to ministry was crystallized. The occasion was a prayer meeting. Pastor Lewis had asked for prayer while he was preaching a revival. An Air Force lieutenant had asked me to join a small group for prayer during the revival (I was a lowly airman). We prayed for hours, though the passing of time was not evident to me. There was only prayer—no preaching, teaching, or singing. Only a few people even prayed out loud and these prayers were tame Baptist type prayers. During that prayer meeting I had the experience of being called into the ministry. I would now describe it as a "baptism of the Holy Spirit", although at the time I was unfamiliar with that term. To me the Lord Jesus baptized me in or with the Holy Spirit. There were no charismatic gifts involved at all, only intense, heartfelt prayer. I was never the same afterward. Now I had a strong desire to share the story of Jesus with others.

Not long after the prayer meeting, the pastor asked me to preach for him at the local juvenile hall (the Solano County facility in Fairfield). I was surprised the pastor even knew who I was. I went and fearfully preached to a packed room of kids, then gave a standard invitation. Some twenty-six kids expressed a desire to trust in Jesus. All my previous attempts at witnessing had been met with either rejection or a lack of an outward, immediate response. What a difference! (For more on the subject of the baptism of the Holy Spirit I recommend *Joy Unspeakable: Power and Renewal in the*

*Holy Spirit* by D. Martyn Lloyd-Jones, Harold Shaw Publishers: Wheaton, Illinois, 1984).

There are many ways to preach the gospel. My personal forum has been to pastor a church. I have often said, "I pastor a church in order to preach the gospel." Miller Avenue Baptist Church is a small church and, at present, I don't have a lot of people to preach to. However, I have sought out creative ways to preach the gospel to a wider audience. I'm encouraged to think that, on any given Sunday morning or evening, maybe one or two non-Christians will be in attendance. Certainly I do not know if someone is born again or not, so even if we have a small attendance there might be people who are not yet converted. And besides, I know that hearing the gospel story is always an encouragement no matter how long a person has been a Christian. I personally love to hear the gospel preached by other people. I may have preached it thousands of times myself, and yet I love to hear the story told again and again. It encourages and strengthens and lifts up more than any other message I know.

I have never apologized for being a preacher of the gospel. When people ask me what I do I tell them, "I am a gospel preacher. I present the message of Jesus, and that's what I do." This is what I was called to do in 1965, as far as I understand it. Whether or not my particular call is general or very unordinary I can't say. I've talked to ministers who have had very specific calls; I've talked to others who have had calls that were more general like my own. But the one element that is common to all calls to pastoral ministry is a desire and drive to preach the gospel, because anything less will not be strong enough when the difficult times come.

✤　✤　✤　✤　✤

☞ Have you been able to satisfy yourself about your own calling?

☞ How might you help someone else who was unsure?

# Three

# Examine Yourself

"I am retiring in less than a year and then I am finished with church for good." This pastor knew he was not a Christian though the members of his congregation did not know it. He did not need to examine himself.

A former colleague in the ministry, a person I had actually recommended for ordination, suddenly resigned his church. He had come to the conclusion he was not really a Christian.

Another pastor, and close friend of mine, was converted after being in the ministry for nearly twenty years.

Sadly, stories such as these are hardly unique. The fact that someone might go into the ministry or be in the ministry already and not be genuinely converted is the reason this chapter comes so close to the beginning of the book.

We must be sure of our own conversion. The Apostle Paul, in 2 Corinthians 13:5, said, "Examine yourselves to see whether you are in the faith; test yourselves. Do you not realize that Jesus

Christ is in you—unless, of course, you have failed the test?"

I love to read of the three Great Awakenings in America. One of the preachers of the First Great Awakening, Gilbert Tennant, published a sermon titled, "The Danger of An Unconverted Ministry". In his day, the Half-Way Covenant, which developed in the 17th Century, was wide spread. This covenant was popularized in New England by Jonathan Edward's grandfather, Solomon Stoddard. The Half-Way Covenant said, in part, that it was not necessary to show evidence of conversion in order to be baptized, to receive communion, to be a member of a church, or to be a minister. Therefore, many of those who occupied the pulpits of churches in 18th Century Colonial America were unconverted. When Tennant preached his sermon he upset many a minister.

The fact is that many of the ministers in Colonial America were not converted; they did not have to show evidence of conversion in order to be ordained to the pastoral ministry. The ministry was often looked upon as just another career choice.

The same occurs in our day as well. And because of the possibility of false conversion, preachers must apply the Corinthians passage to themselves. I have written a book called, *Are You Really Born Again?* (Evangelical Press, 1998), that deals extensively with false conversion. The book discusses the process of "Christianization"—how someone can look and sound like a Christian but not really being one, and how someone can have profound religious and spiritual experiences yet remain unconverted.

To be engaged in pastoral ministry and yet be unconverted—this is a great tragedy. Many think they are converted on the basis of church membership, baptism, good deeds, holding to orthodox creeds and doctrine, and so on. In fact, some mistakenly believe they are truly converted because they are ministers.

Those pursuing the pastoral ministry should examine themselves to see if they have been truly converted. The following questions might facilitate such an examination: Did you sense of a need for forgiveness? Were you aware of your separation and alienation from God? Did you realize that unless your sin was forgiven you had no hope? Did you understand that Jesus' shed blood is the only means for forgiveness of sin? Is Jesus your only hope for eternal life? Do you desire to turn from sin in repentance? Is Jesus your object of trust for salvation? If so, as the Puritan preachers would say, conversion has "hopefully" taken place.

Or, on the other hand, did you merely experience a desire to stop sinning and become a better person? Did you decide to become more spiritual and observe religious commandments? Did you rely upon you own goodness? Did you hope that actions done in the name of God would suffice? Did a crisis provoke a life-style change that incorporated some kind of religious philosophy? Did you form a bond to a spiritual community coupled with a subsequent adherence to a religious viewpoint? If so, then it may be true that "christianization" has taken place instead of true conversion.

These questions must be faced sincerely and in a straightforward manner. No preacher wants to stand at The Great Judgement and hear Jesus say, "Depart from me, I never knew you."

Yes, it is possible for an unconverted minister to preach the gospel and see persons genuinely converted. How is this possible? God honors the preaching of His

Word. Faith comes through the proclamation of the gospel; even the stones could cry out the message. Good works done in the name of God, by even "good" people, are ineffectual to secure salvation.

In accordance with the Scripture then, you must examine yourself. Don't settle for anything other than simple trusting Jesus for salvation and knowing that Jesus alone is the source of forgiveness and righteousness.

If you recognize that you have not been truly converted, I suggest you wrestle with God until assurance comes. Assurance does not consist in having lived a perfect life where there are no doubts, temptations, and actual sin. Assurance comes when your trust is in Jesus and His shed blood. There is a knowing certainty that the Holy Spirit brings, although it need not be overpowering or dramatic. Rather, it is often a peaceful reliance upon Jesus alone for salvation.

☞ Have you ever examined your own conversion?

☞ What did you find?

☞ Have you ever asked someone else, for their own best interest, to examine their conversion to see if it was genuine or not?

☞ Does this seem brash, arrogant, or even unnecessary?

## Four

# Pastoring To Preach

"I would never say I am a preacher. I am a minister and my job is to be a pastor."

I agreed with my friend readily enough; my favorite title is "pastor," yet I like to say that I am first and foremost a preacher. It is an old-time word to be sure, and there were some years when I shunned the designation. But now I like to say I am a preacher.

✢    ✢    ✢    ✢    ✢

In the second chapter I said that I pastored a church in order to preach the gospel. I would like to elaborate on that theme.

First I should say that a pastor must have the desire to care for and love others. A pastor must be able to empathize with people in their struggle and striving to grow up into the stature of the fullness of Jesus. A pastor must be willing to either personally be engaged in meeting the congregation's spiritual needs or ensure that such ministry is available from others.

The Apostle Paul's instruction to Timothy, who functioned in pastoral ministry in addition to other responsibilities, includes the following:

"In the presence of God and of Christ Jesus, who will judge the living and the dead, and in view of his appearing and his kingdom, I give

19

you this charge: Preach the Word; be prepared in season and out of season; correct, rebuke and encourage—with great patience and careful instruction." (2 Timothy 4:1-2)

These words might be appropriately applied to pastoral ministry, which is the caring for God's people in a local church setting. Paul begins his charge with "Preach the Word."

I believe this is significant.

I am not necessarily very good at being a pastor. On a scale of one to ten (one being a very poor pastor and ten a very excellent pastor) I would give myself a four—somewhat under average. I don't say this to be cute, clever, or immodest. This is just the truth of it and I have not hidden this from the congregation. I depend upon others to help me in pastoral ministry. I am not a good visitor; I don't like going to hospitals; I do not like ministerial meetings; and I do not like meeting with committees. Of course I do these things, but I hope others in the church will make up for my lack.

To a considerable degree then, I pastor in order to preach the gospel. I have a responsibility to present the gospel to as large a segment of my community as I can, and I employ various means to accomplish this goal.

For the past sixteen years I have produced a community access television program called *The Bible Study*. I simply sit in front of two cameras, one a close-up the other a long shot, and work my way verse by verse through the Bible. There is no editing. If I cough or sneeze or burp or whatever else, there is no editing. This allows me to film four programs in one afternoon a month. It doesn't cost me any money, and most communities have this same access through local cable companies. Almost every day I run into someone who mentions the program. People that I have never known stop me on the street. And it gives me a little extra-added opportunity to preach the gospel. It is a very simple thing; I don't rant and rave and I never ask for money. It is simply a verse by verse Bible exposition.

And then, since 1986, I host workshops. For these last fourteen years, a number of volunteers and I have conducted a Divorce Recovery and Loss Workshop for people who have experienced the ending of a relationship by means of divorce or death. From time to time we also do a Parenting Workshop and a Marriage Workshop. I keep track of the participant's birth dates and on his or her birth date I send out a tape of two of my sermons. I have been surprised at how many people will actually listen to them. It is an additional way of presenting the gospel.

And then there the many couples I have married over the years. It is quite a long list now, and I keep track of the wedding dates. Before the anniversary date I send out a sermon tape. So I minister to, in terms of sending out the tapes, a congregation (if it might be called this), that is probably twenty times larger than Miller Avenue's.

Miller Avenue's website, WWW.W3CHURCH.ORG, opens up a worldwide ministry. Through the website we present the gospel, offer sermon tapes, and make other materials available.

These are all simple and cost effective ministries that are feasible for small churches. Most preachers can do a community access television program. A tape ministry is rather easy to begin. Building a website is within the reach of any church. The American Bible Society, in fact, has provided a website for every church in North America. All that is needed is to type into a locator WWW.HOUSESOFWORSHIP.NET and find a church's website. Most every church has one ready and waiting. (If the church is not listed a request may be made to the Society for inclusion.)

There is much more including jail ministries. I have volunteered at San Quentin State Prison for many years going back to 1968 though not continuously. For the last fourteen years I have been part of the *Prison Bible Studies* and have been able to go cell to cell in the blocks. Our church holds periodic worship services at the Protestant, Garden Chapel. And for the last four years I have co-coached the prison's baseball team. There are convalescent hospitals, rescue missions, homeless outreaches; a pastor will find creative ways to reach the unconverted and provide opportunities for others in the church family to do the same.

Preaching the gospel is central to being a faithful pastor. While you may prefer other facets of ministry, a pastor can not neglect this vital responsibility. The charge to preach the gospel is clear and the opportunities are endless.

☞ Are you comfortable with the designation "preacher" for yourself?

☞ Are there particular images it invokes for you?

☞ How would you rate yourself as a pastor?

☞ How would you rate yourself as a preacher of the gospel?

Five

# Preparation for the Pastoral Ministry

"All I need is a Bible. Why do you waste your time going to school?"

"If you've got the Spirit you don't need all those books I see on your shelf."

I understood the young men who made these comments. They were recent converts and very zealous. But they were not wise.

✣　✣　✣　✣　✣

The Scripture is clear: "Do your best to present yourself to God as one approved, a workman who does not need to be ashamed and who correctly handles the word of truth" (2 Timothy 2:15). This is what Paul told Timothy. And we will be ashamed unless we adequately prepare ourselves for ministry.

Traditionally the main line denominations have expected a formal education in terms of a bachelor's degree and seminary training on top of that. And this is no doubt preferable. The kinds of disciplines that are learned in the process of a rather rigorous education will stand a pastor in good stead as time goes by. Much of a pastor's time is spent preparing messages, sermons, and teachings; this requires a great deal of study and research—patient, disciplined scholarship. These are facts.

Personally, I spent five years in college trying to earn a four-year degree. Following that, I spent ten years in two different seminaries: Golden Gate Baptist Theological Seminary for six years, and four years at the San Francisco Theological Seminary. The first was a Southern Baptist institution, the second a Presbyterian. And those years were not wasted. I learned how to study; I learned how to read. I learned how to listen to others and take notes. I learned how to evaluate the opinions of other people who where more advanced in their knowledge and experience. I had the opportunity of engaging in dialogue, debate, and controversy with other students. And I had the opportunity of learning to put my thoughts down on paper on a regular basis.

These are tremendous advantages for anyone who would spend their life communicating, and so much of the pastoral ministry is just that—communication. The preacher has the Word of God, the gospel message, and all of the fullness of the Scripture to communicate to others. Sometimes the communicating is to non-believers, sometimes to believers; but it's communication, whether it's preaching, teaching, writing a newsletter, or preparing the Sunday bulletin. All of these are vehicles of communication, and a good education can only help.

Pastors must be a scholars their entire life. Let me briefly describe how I continue my education.

The languages of the Scripture, Greek and Hebrew, are special to me. In seminary I took some advanced Greek classes and I have continued to study both languages. My practice is to study actual texts and do some translating; I read verses aloud in the original languages, and study grammar books.

A minister should like grammar books. When I find a good grammar book of almost any language I'll pick it up. I have Greek, Hebrew, German, Latin, Spanish, and English grammar books in my little library, and although they are not tremendously exciting to read, they are instructive. I also attempt to keep up a study of Latin and Spanish.

The pastor who loves to read is blessed indeed. There are periods of time when I will focus on one particular area. For example, I have spent a year or so reading astrophysics. I spent another year or more working in the area of microbiology. At one point I read a number of books on biology. Another time I focused on finance and economics; I was interested in the stock market. World history has always held a fascination for me. I particularly like political essays, wherever I can find them. Magazines and journals like *Time*, *Newsweek*, the *Smithsonian*, and *Discover* are favorites. I am fascinated with paleontology. Each morning I read the local newspaper thoroughly. From time to time I will take a class or attend a seminar or hear a special speaker at one of the seminaries. Journals, newspapers, and newsletters from all over the world will arrive at my mailbox during the course of the year and there is much in them to learn from.

But what about individuals who do not have the opportunity to attend formal institutions of education, is there a place for them? Well, of course, there is. I know several ministers who have had long and significant pastoral ministries who are essentially self-taught people, self-taught in the sense that they did not receive a formal education. (Mark Buckley who wrote a foreword for this book is such a person.) But they became students on their own, they loved the Scripture, they loved to talk with people who were more informed, and they acquired mentors—people who could instruct them.

I have served as a mentor for a number of people over the course of my years; that is, I suggested various topics to study and monitored the progress. I've worked with people who have spent a year or so in, for example, church history, reading a number of volumes in that field, and then they would move to the Old Testament or the New Testament. I've known people who have studied Greek and Hebrew, learned it on their own. I have taught both of those languages one on one for people who had no opportunity to learn any other way because of work and family obligations.

Therefore my experience has taught me that it is not impossible to acquire a good education apart from an institutional setting, but it does require discipline. There is really no place in the pastoral ministry for one who is lazy. We recall that slothfulness is a sin, and it is a great sin for a pastor. While enrolled in a doctoral program and being required to keep track of how I spent my time, I discovered my workweek was just under ninety hours. This, of course, was excessive and I corrected the error. However, it is an indication that the life of the pastor is a busy one. And it is necessary that the pastor become a disciplined scholar and learner.

One of the best ways for an individual to prepare for ministry, when they have not the opportunity to either acquire a formal education (or even if they have), or secure a formal mentoring relationship, is to seek out a local pastor—someone with considerable experience—who would be willing to work with an earnest volunteer. I have imagined myself a young man starting out, say in my mid-twenties, wanting to learn to be a pastor but having no opportunity for a formal education. I would look for someone who had not less than ten years experience in the ministry, and was at least 40 years of age--preferably older. I imagined myself becoming a "gofer"— someone who did the little things that the pastor would do but didn't have the time to do. I would be at church early, set up, clean up, stay late, and put everything away and clean up again. I would observe, I would listen, I would take notes, and I would see how the ministry was actually carried out. My goal would be to be as invisible as possible and not be a problem. And I would hope to gradually accept small responsibilities. Perhaps I would be handing out bulletins on Sunday morning, perhaps serving as a usher, perhaps working in a Sunday school in some capacity, perhaps singing in the choir, perhaps reading a Scripture on Sunday morning, perhaps visiting people who the pastor had not opportunity or time to visit. I would avoid making suggestions, never critique, but always seek to be a faithful, loyal participant. I think that is what I would do. I would, perhaps, ask for suggestions for reading and ask for opportunities to discuss the material--but without having any expectations. I would hope to learn what it is to be a servant.

The reason I emphasized being a servant is because a person who is not willing to be a servant will never make it in the pastoral ministry. The pastoral ministry is primarily servanthood; the pastor is the chief servant in a congregation. The individual who is looking for a place of leadership, a place of power and authority, a place of recognition, will not long survive in the pastoral ministry, or at least, would not have a significant ministry over the long haul.

No one is ever completely prepared for the pastoral ministry. In my thirties I thought that by the time I was forty I would be equipped. Then in my forties I thought that by my fifties I would be really confident in my work. Shall I think that by my sixties I will be where I want to be? No, I will not look to my sixties because I know better now. I will never get to a place where I am competent and content. No, I must go with what I have now while striving to grow in grace and knowledge. The job is bigger than I am, but I am confident, however, that the Holy Spirit of God will do what I can not.

☞ Equipped and ready to go—this is how we would like to feel. Have you ever felt so confident?

☞ What are you doing to prepare yourself?

# Six

# The Devotional Life

"I haven't read my Bible in months and I sure don't have time to pray." These words were from my own mouth, a confession I did not want to make. And at the time I was pastor of a church and would commonly "exhort" others to pray and read their Bibles. Did I ever feel like a hypocrite!

✠　✠　✠　✠　✠

A consistent devotional life is as essential for a pastor as it is for any Christian. This seems only too obvious, but pastors will neglect devotional and other spiritual disciplines reasoning that they get all they need through sermon and Bible study preparation. However, preparation for public ministry and devotional disciplines are to be distinguished. There, of course, will be overlap, but the time spent with Jesus in prayer and Bible study is essential for building our relationship with Him.

The Christian life is a relationship, and the devotional life is perhaps the measure of that relationship. By devotional life I mean prayer; I mean the study of the Scripture, reflection upon the doctrines of Scripture and upon the gospel; it is a focusing on God and His Word. And it is in that relationship we have with God that ministry emerges.

29

A satisfying and meaningful devotional life, though, does not come easily.

It has often been said that we can not give away what we do not have. And there is some truth to that, but it is not the reason we have a devotional life. If I am empty inside I can still preach and teach. The power of the gospel is in the Word and Spirit, but I want to have a close personal relationship with Jesus for His sake alone. We love God for who He is and because He loves us. It is tainted "love" that expects anything in return. Whether we abound or are in need, whether we live or die, we learn to love the Lord God for His steadfast love and grace alone.

Study of the Scripture was something I loved from the beginning and it has been a big part of my life. Prayer is regularly a struggle. This is not altogether true for I recall several years, during the seventies, when I loved to pray and would do so for hours at a time. In a way, I can measure the strength of my relationship with God by looking at my prayer life.

During the most productive times of my life I would spend an hour or more, sometimes several hours a day, in the pursuit of my devotional disciplines. My most productive time as a writer, for instance, (a short space of time in the 1970's) coincided with a strong and consistent devotional life.

But what happens in the hurried pace of pastoral ministry, the press of people, family responsibilities—these and other demands on our time? The answer is we neglect being alone with Jesus. When the pressure comes in the form of writing letters, answering and returning phone calls, preparing messages, outlining Bible studies, attending meetings, finishing reports—these "priorities" take over. And, in the small church especially, there is no one else around to do this important work.

Let me say it again, there is no end to the pastoral ministry, never a time when we can say, "This job is over." The work, even in a small church, can be overwhelming and soon the time spent with the Lord is gone. And I say this because I am one who has often ignored the devotional life in order to get the more practical aspects of the work done. I know that to be a mistake. I end up regretting it though I'm conscious that I'm doing it. I give myself little excuses. "I'll get back to it." "This is temporary." "I'll do it later tonight." This last notion is a complete delusion since I am aware that my devotional time has got to be in the morning or it will not be there at all. Once I get very far into the day, the press of people and events and circumstances take over.

What is the solution? I have no simple answer, but I will describe briefly how I cope. As early in the day as possible I read my Bible and pray. If I am interrupted, well, that is that. I will not fall into guilt about it. That is the worst, allowing guilt to motivate my devotional life. If I get interrupted, I will go back to it if I can. But Jesus loves me whether I spend time with Him in secret or not. That is the key, security in the relationship. He is mine and I am His. Nothing can change that fact.

Finding someplace to be quiet and shielded from the telephone, computer, and people knocking on the door—this is what I must have, even if it is for only fifteen or twenty minutes. If I have more time, that is better. But the devotional life, that time spent with Jesus, is the very best time of my day.

In the next chapter, I will again deal with this most important subject and speak of it in a somewhat different way.

✢    ✢    ✢    ✢    ✢

☞ Are you satisfied or frustrated with the quality of your devotional life?

☞ If frustrated, are you sometimes overcome with guilt?

☞ How might you as a pastor encourage a person who struggled in this way?

Seven

# The Center of Our Ministry— Abiding in Jesus

"I feel as cold and hard as a piece of steel buried under a glacier at the North Pole. I'm a professional all right, I've been trained to do and I do it. I don't feel a thing."

A pastor who at one time was "on fire for the Lord" spoke these words to me. My efforts to encourage him were to no avail; in a few years he was out of the ministry completely.

✠    ✠    ✠    ✠    ✠

Christianity is a personal relationship, a saving relationship, with Jesus, our Lord and Savior. The heart of the relationship may be expressed as, "spending time with Jesus". Study of the Bible, prayer, and other spiritual exercises essentially are means of spending time with or fellowshipping with the Father, the Son, and the Holy Spirit.

All Christian work, activity, or ministry must flow out of the relationship with Jesus, especially the preaching of the gospel and the teaching of the Bible.

One of my favorite ways of stating the nature of the relationship we have with Jesus is "*abiding in Christ*". Jesus said, "If you abide in me and I abide in you, you will bear much fruit" (John 15:5, author's paraphrase). To abide in Jesus is to remain in Him, trust, and submit to Him, surrender to Him as Lord. Christians throughout the history of the Church have found this to be a perfectly reliable truth. Our abiding in Jesus and His abiding in us—this is the Christian life.

It must be confessed that I am not altogether sure what it means "to abide in Christ". I believe, though, that it means to rest in Him and trust that He is all of our righteousness, that there is no work that we are required to do in order to gain His acceptance or love. It means, in addition, that by the inward working of the Holy Spirit we enter into the finished work of Jesus in all its fullness. That completed work of forgiveness and salvation is imputed to us or placed within us as a free work of God's sovereign grace. We have no righteousness of our own, none at all. Any righteousness I may cling to is akin to filthy rags. I have to admit that my heart is desperately wicked and corrupt, even deceitful to the point I deceive myself. Only by the light of God's Spirit am I able to see that I am thoroughly corrupt. I am a person such as Peter who said: "Go away from me, Lord; I am a sinful man" (Luke 5:8)! Now, by the inexhaustible riches of His grace, we are in Him and He is in us. And still I have no righteousness of my own; rather I am completely dependent on the finished work of Jesus. I am then invited by Jesus to abide in Him.

Jesus has called us into His ministry, called us to pastor, shepherd, and feed His flock. It is not something that we have necessarily chosen for ourselves, but due to the prompting of the Holy Spirit we have entered into a partnership ministry with Jesus. And so it is His work and He must and will equip us to do it. For me this means abiding in Him, resting in Him, looking to Him for every provision for the accomplishment of the task that He has set before me.

We are called *to abide in Jesus*, this *is* our ministry.

✦     ✦     ✦     ✦     ✦

☞ Do you have another way of expressing the subject of this chapter?

☞ Does "abiding in Jesus" seem illusive or intangible to you?

Eight

# Remember, We Have a Fallen Nature

"Kent, you can't talk me out of it. I've failed for the last time. I don't deserve to be a pastor. I'm finished."

And he was finished. Though I tried, I could not reach him. His "failure", for most people, would not seem so very serious, but to him it was unforgivable. It wasn't that God could not forgive him, he could not forgive himself.

✠    ✠    ✠    ✠    ✠

Every minister of the gospel must be aware that there is a corruption within. Not only do we have a fallen nature, sin (as well as Satan) is crouching at the door like a lion ready to pounce on us, chew us up, and spit us out. It is a great mistake to deny this fact.

A pastor is vulnerable to gross sin, and is presented with more than the routine share of opportunities to grievous sin. For instance, it is possible to embezzle, misappropriate, and misuse money that has been entrusted into the care of the church. Pastors do have a fiduciary duty over the tithes and offerings, both in terms of receiving and spending the money.

One day I returned to the church office discouraged about money or rather the lack of it. Four days remained before pay day and my kids badly needed tennis shoes. Stuck under the door was an envelope that turned out to contain two twenty-dollar bills. An accompanying note read: "For the church."

I took the money and bought the tennis shoes. Though glad to take care of my little girls, I was plagued with guilt. As soon as I got paid, I replaced the money, but my taking the money in the first place was wrong.

Pastors may not only steal money directly or engage in embezzling to violate their trust. They might also channel money into pet projects by the use of manipulative tactics. I have done this many times and always for "good" reasons. It may be a worthy mission project or a sound system that would vastly improve the quality of the music. The point is the pastor pushes it strongly and shames people into assenting to the proposal. Without the pastoral pressure, the project would never have moved forward. This may be a case of unfair manipulation.

Most pastors of small churches work alongside pastors of big churches who receive large salaries. The pastor of the smaller church and/or smaller salary may be tempted to jealousy and envy. Few church members would imagine that their pastor might harbor a desire to keep up with Rev. Jones down the block. However, pastors will, and pastors do. The point is jealousy and/or envy might be a stimulus for questionable or downright sinful money management.

Another area where we must remember we have a fallen nature is in regard to sex. Very few escape this one, if not in actuality then in thought and imagination. The sexual drive is a powerful force.

The following is one reason pastors get into adulterous situations. People are attracted to people in power, and a pastor is often viewed as an individual with power. However humble a servant might be, the process of making public presentations invests a certain amount of power and authority in the preacher. Standing and delivering a sermon week after week may be sufficient to attract people in ways that are not healthy.

In addition, pastors relate to people in very personal and intimate ways and will unavoidably establish associations with members of the opposite sex to the point that significant friendships develop. Pastors also become close to people who are in vulnerable circumstances such as when there has been the experience of loss, perhaps through death or divorce. It may be that a pastor attempts to meet needs in ways that are inappropriate or takes advantage of a position of authority. It is not surprising that attractions develop; however, an adulterous situation may be the result.

The pastoral ministry can be, and most often is, quite stressful. Certain diversions seem to hold promise of stress reduction. Those things that we would not do, we do. Those things that we would do, we do not do. Paul is very clear about the situation in the 7th Chapter of Romans. We are vulnerable! We may stand and preach against fornication, adultery, and all forms of sexual immorality, yet find ourselves falling victim to it not long after. We need to realize that sin is crouching at the door and that Satan goes around like a roaring lion looking for someone to devour.

From time to time there appears in the news media the story of a professional athlete who is arrested for solicitation, drunkenness, fighting, drug abuse, and so on, immediately following the athletic contest. Stage performers, similarly, have found their names in the newspapers for an unlawful incident, which often occurs right after a brilliant performance. Preachers, too, often get into trouble after the service, Bible study, or prayer meeting is over. Why?

Though preaching, teaching, and worship leading are not athletic contests or performances, they nonetheless involve being before "audiences". There can be an accompanying stimulation, an adrenaline rush, which can be intoxicating. When the "event" is concluded, discouragement, depression, despondency, even a powerful drive for "carnality" may surface. To put it another way, an emotional vulnerability may be created after being before an "audience". I do not know why this is but I have experienced it many times myself. This "syndrome" has been present whether I have preached a good sermon or a bad sermon. Additionally, I have talked with other pastors who have told me they are most tempted by sin on Sunday night after all the ministry is over. Even Charles Spurgeon would suffer terrible bouts of depression after preaching. This "syndrome" is very common but little spoken of or understood. Therefore, pastors beware, after the preaching, sin is crouching at the door. Make plans accordingly. If you need to be with people, do so, arrange for it. If you need peace and solitude, see to it. Whatever works, figure it out and make the proper application.

A high percentage of pastors fall pray to sexual sin. And when a pastor does fall it is a rare individual who is able to survive and come back. Some can, some do, and it would be hoped that they could, but it is often the case that that is the end of a ministry.

Substance abuse is found among pastors, too. Alcohol is the most common substance abused by pastors since there is a certain acceptability about drinking alcoholic beverages. Drugs, prescription and otherwise, have also found their way into pastor's lives.

I have seen addiction to crack cocaine and heroin in the pastoral ministry. The stress pastors invariably experience may account for or contribute to substance abuse. It happens! We have a corrupt heart, a fallen nature. Anything is possible.

What is a pastor to do who stumbles or falls? An adequate answer would require an enormous volume of material, however, I would suggest seeking Jesus and His righteousness first; abide in Jesus and do not lean on the flesh. Then pray for true repentance. Also, seek help from someone else, a person who can bring an objective viewpoint and expertise to the situation. Step out of ministry for a time if necessary, perhaps for a lengthy period of time. It is not necessary to inform the entire church of the circumstances, but if the problems persist, it is wise to withdraw as cleanly as possible. There is always hope, there is always healing, there is always grace, mercy, and forgiveness.

Pastors are not super people magically shielded from the world, the flesh, and the devil. *We are vulnerable*! We can easily be transgressors of laws that we want to uphold, and I think we are especially vulnerable when we do not realize our limitations. Remember, we have a fallen nature!

Grace is so very wonderful. Experiencing God's grace for ourselves helps us share it with others.

☞ Is there a particular episode in your life that you can use as an illustration of God's amazing grace in a sermon?

Nine

# On Learning to Preach

"You sound just like Billy Graham, Tommy," I said. He grinned, "You know, I think I do."

Tommy was my next door neighbor at Golden Gate Baptist Theological Seminary in Mill Valley. After hearing him preach in our homiletics class I said, "Tommy, would you preach a revival at my church?"

He did preach the revival, a few new people attended the first service, but it was not very successful. Tommy preached like Billy Graham all right but it didn't seem to help. And we didn't know why.

✠ ✠ ✠ ✠ ✠

Billy Graham—the preacher us seminary students wanted to be like. Some of us felt that if we could preach like Billy Graham we might be as effective, not to mention well known, as he was. When I started pastoring in 1966 I tried my best to preach like the great evangelist. Though I thought I copied him pretty well, the church did not fill up. This is a bit of an exaggeration of course, but I really did think that if I preached and gave an invitation like Billy Graham, why, of course, the church would fill up.

Readers: Do not rush to Miller Avenue to hear me preach. I consider myself an average preacher. On a scale of one to ten I think I am about a four. However, I like to think I am getting better as time goes on. I am unsure of that, but I like to think that is true. In any case, here on some ideas on preaching.

*Preaching needs to be clear.* Clarity is a major key to preaching. Make it plain! Make it understandable! And this is not easily done. Biblical doctrines can be complex, and they need to be explained carefully. Complicated and sophisticated theologies and doctrines may be presented in an intellectual manner, but the average listener should be able to understand the message. It is not that people are illiterate, although that may be true in some cases, but I encourage the preacher to have in mind the person who does not have a solid grasp of the Bible and theology. Some of the more biblically literate people in the congregation may be bored from time to time, but clarity is extremely important.

A current trend is to avoid the preaching of doctrine and theology. This is not the same as the need for clarity. Sound bites, infomercials, about the so-called real life problems—this is advocated by many. It is thought that doctrinal preaching goes over the head of most people so give them what they are used to—the television format geared to twelve-year-olds. The gospel preacher must reject such nonsense or the people will indeed remain illiterate. I have found that people love to get into the complex theologies, they even like to learn some Greek and Hebrew, and want to be conversant with church history and the great heroes of the faith. Don't preach down, preach up to the people of God. Treat them like adults who have the hunger and capacity to grasp the great doctrines. They get plenty of the pop psychology through the media as it is. Somebody is always giving them advice on how to be successful, prosperous, and happy. The preacher deals with the timeless, ultimate questions, and issues. Refuse to become a "contemporary" preacher.

*Preaching must be with sufficient volume so that everyone can hear.* Far too often, even when microphones are being used, the preacher cannot be heard. Some preachers simply do not know how to use a microphone! A microphone will be in place, yet preachers will not speak into it. They will either stand too far back or they will walk around leaving the microphone ineffective.

Part of the aging process can be a loss of hearing, generally speaking. This is certainly true in my case; I have a hearing loss in both ears, and I do not like it when I cannot hear or I have to strain in order to make out the words. I prefer loud! Loud is better than soft! Now you can preach softly if there is good amplification, but that system must be used properly. A lapel microphone is quite useful, that way if the preacher moves around the preaching is still audible.

The small church pastor might learn to preach without any amplification at all. In fact, let me suggest it. Learn not to rely on a microphone if at all possible. For some people who have small voices I have urged them to sing in a choir or acquire a voice teacher and learn how to build up speaking volume. What did the preachers do before the modern age? They spoke up, developed wind and strength, and could often be heard for surprising distances.

*Preaching must be intense*! I cannot listen to someone who does not appear to be genuinely concerned about what they are saying. This does not mean a performance, but the preacher of the gospel must have a sense of the importance of the message. That cannot be simulated. It is either there or it is not. Acting can not make up for genuine intensity.

Some have taught that preaching should be like normal conversation. "Preach like you talk," is the advice. I disagree! Preaching is not the same as conversation. Preaching needs both heat and light. When we present the truth of the Word of God (light) it should be impassioned (heat). Conversation is casual, preaching is not, it is ultimate communication. By this I do not mean shouting or acting. The people in the pew know what is genuine and what is not, and they can "feel" the heat.

*Preaching must be courageous.* It is not easy to call sin "sin" and clearly point out that "sinners are in the hands of an angry God". It takes courage to preach the gospel to smug, self-righteous people.

It is love that must motivate the preacher, love that warns and pleads. One person in particular comes to mind. A peaceful, sensitive, and generous man, he actively pursued a deeper devotion to God. However he had no conversion testimony, had not, by his own account, trusted in Jesus as Savior and/or Lord. In some ways his devout and spiritual life-style intimidated me, but I suspected he was unconverted and it was not easy for me to tell him so. Had I not been given the courage to be honest the man might have remained unconverted.

Before moving to the next point, let me emphasize two points only hinted at in the above paragraph. One, the preacher must have the courage to contend for the salvation of sinners.

"Compel Them to Come In" is the title of my favorite Spurgeon sermon. It is an earnest appeal for sinners to trust in Jesus from the "Prince of Preachers". Spurgeon pleads as an ambassador for Christ for people to be reconciled to God. He pleads! It seems as though there are tears in his eyes. His love for Jesus and for those whom Jesus died marks the sermon from beginning to end. (This sermon can be emailed to you.)

Preachers of the gospel may indeed plead with sinners to come to Jesus in a genuine way because the preacher will love sinners and not want to see them lost forever. I have not always been this way, I will admit, but there are times when it is so with me. This is how I want it to be and it comes when the Holy Spirit shows me the great love God the Father has for those who have rebelled against Him.

Two, the preacher must continue though the preaching is going badly. I have lost my confidence as a preacher a number of times. There have been extended times when I could not preach well at all. During those times I could see the pained expressions on the faces of the people; even my staunchest supporters sent me notes saying they were praying for me.

A baseball analogy has helped me when I am in such a miserable place. I know that baseball players can lose confidence in their ability to hit a baseball. The solution is to keep swinging the bat; the batter in a slump keeps stepping up to the plate. I do the same, I keep preaching, but I go back to the basics. In a preaching slump I will preach nothing but expository sermons, verse by verse messages directly from the Scripture. I will go to my favorite chapter, my favorite parable, my favorite verse—and preach away. If necessary, I will sit down with my Bible and start reading until some passage grabs me and then I will study it diligently until I have so much material I'll never get it all said. Sometimes I've gone back and looked at sermon outlines I knew I had preached well and tried them again. I keep preaching until I preach myself out of the slump. And this requires a great deal of courage. These days I am not surprised when I find myself in a preaching slump, in fact, I am in one right now. I hate it, but I am not going to panic, whine, complain, or blame some circumstance. Preachers never give up.

*Preachers must not settle for mere "Christianization."*Christianization is the taking on or assuming of doctrines, behavior, and speech that are identified with Christianity when in fact, there is no true conversion. This is more common, I believe, than most pastors realize. For twenty-nine years I did not realize the phenomenon was so powerful and widespread. I assumed that if a person talked, acted, and "believed" like a Christian then who was I to doubt or question it. I would settle for christianization.

It is not enough that a person believes that Jesus died on the cross for sin and that He rose again the third day. It is not enough that a person sign their name to a statement that they believe 100% in the Apostles' Creed. Doctrinal belief is not the same as true conversion. The demons even know these things and they "shudder". (see James 2:19)

It is not enough that a person copies or simulates Christian expressions and conversation, even worship styles and praise. Mimicking things Christian does not a disciple make. Many non-Christians praise and worship all manner of gods and goddesses, including (they suppose) the God of Scripture, often with great devotion and sincerity.

It is not enough that a person experience "miracles" and "gifts" supposedly from God. Since the devil imitates the genuine gifts of God it is not helpful to assume that all spiritual phenomenon originate with the Holy Spirit. Satan does work signs and wonders, and they are powerfully deceptive.

It is not enough that a person is a church member, has been baptized, and receives communion regularly. These are works that a Christian does out of obedience to the commands of God and in order to honor Him as Lord. They do not produce conversion.

The gospel preacher presents Jesus and invites people to trust in Him as Savior. We need not be quick to confirm conversion. People will struggle under the conviction of the Holy Spirit; there may be considerable turmoil. I am reminded of the excruciating conversion experiences of Augustine, Martin Luther, George Whitefield, John Wesley, and John Newton among others. The Holy Spirit will confirm a person's salvation; they will know when they are converted having been persuaded by God Himself that they are His children. (see Romans 8:16, 2 Corinthians 1:22, Ephesians 1:13 and 2 Timothy 1:12)

*Beginning preachers can seek out experienced preachers who will honestly critique their preaching.* If a person can not accept criticism when it comes to preaching, then that person should examine the call to ministry. Yes, I am willing to put it in this way. A person who is so sensitive and vulnerable that the prospect of an evaluation of a sermon results in fear or defensiveness is not ready to preach.

Preaching is something that is never mastered. I have been preaching for more than three decades and I am very aware of my inadequacies. And it is not only style and presentation I am thinking of. It is more now that I am concerned that I will not be able to present Jesus and His gospel the way I should. Now I am more aware than ever that I am accountable to God for my ministry and it is an awesome prospect. Therefore, I want to be the best preacher I can be and part of that means getting help with the preaching. And what better process could one employ than that of asking an experienced preached for evaluation and critique.

Admittedly this is not easily done, but here are some suggestions. One, tape a sermon and ask another preacher to listen to it. If this works once, do it over and over, spreading tapes around to other preachers. Two, invite a retired preacher to listen to a live sermon. Three, ask a mature member of the congregation to critically examine the preaching; make sure that person is capable of bringing a real critique. Four, tape and listen to your own sermons. Sometimes I shudder at my own preaching and feel discouraged. I tell myself, "I know I am not so wonderful, but that I will do anything to grow and improve."

And finally, *Expect that God's Holy Spirit will bring fruit out of the presentation of Scripture and of the gospel.* The preacher relies upon the Holy Spirit to do this and not upon emotionalism, sad stories, or sentimental poems. I never tell heart-rending stories at the end of sermons, or in the beginning of them nor in the middle. My interest is not in bringing some kind of climatic, emotional conclusion to the sermon, though I will be as persuasive as I can be. Often the conclusions to my sermons are quite abrupt; I just come to the end and announce: "I ask you to believe in the Lord Jesus, I command and compel you to come to Christ." My aim is to leave the sermon in the lap of the hearers. "What will you do now? How has God's Holy Spirit been speaking to you? Are you being drawn to Jesus? Do you want to come to Jesus right now?"

It is the anointing or unction of the Holy Spirit that transforms a talk into a sermon. I believe God's anointing is working as the truth of the gospel of Jesus is presented. People will be drawn to Jesus when He is lifted up. (I recommend *Spirit Empowered Preaching* by Arturo G. Azurdia III, published by Christian Focus Publications of Great Britain.)

Errol Hulse, on December 5, 1998, spoke at the induction of a new pastor for the Welwyn Evangelical Church in Great Britain (as reported in the January 1999 issue of Evangelical Times, page 3.)His exhortation to the new pastor on the subject of preaching hits the mark:

"He is to preach the good news of salvation through Jesus Christ alone. He must use all appropriate means available to him to spread this message, but must not succumb to the modern temptation to compromise either the message or the God-appointed means of making it known.

He must teach and instruct those who are converted. This is not an easy task—it requires energy. His preaching must be expository, systematic, exegetical, doctrinal and experiential. It must be applied to all the various kinds of people who hear him. It must be compelling and relevant. It must be undergirded with prayer."

Iain H. Murray's, <u>*Pentecost-Today?* (Banner of Truth, 1998)</u>, has been a valuable resource for me. Chapter 4 in the book is titled, *"The Holy Spirit and Preaching"*. After reading it I was encouraged afresh to preach in the power of the Holy Spirit so that I might both understand the truth of the Word of God and make it plain to those I preach to.

There are many authoritative voices counseling the adoption of a preaching style designed to attract the baby boomer, and later generations, who have been brought up watching 20 hours of television every week, who have a short attention span, and who are said to neither care for nor know the Bible. Renowned professors of homiletics, in order to attract the television generation, call for sermons that are 12 to 30 minutes in length (30 would be pushing it though) and preaching without notes (only politicians use notes on television). The Bible's use, they say, should be minimized. Of course, a pulpit, where a Bible and sermon notes might be placed, is to be rejected. Sermons should be narrative, that is, a sermon should be like a story—so the Epistles of the New Testament, which are not narrative in style, would not find much use. The preacher does not focus on proclaiming the Good News of the gospel but rather functions as a spiritual director or therapist. "How to" sermons are the most effective; sermon topics should be topical rather than expository (verse by verse teaching and preaching are discouraged). The goal is to speak to peoples "inner person", addressing their immediate psychological, "spiritual", and sociological needs.

Preachers can always learn from those who claim to know how to be successful in our post-modern world. We rely though on the power of the Holy Spirit to apply the Word of God to the heart, soul, and mind of the hearer. Surely it is yet true that, "Faith comes from what is heard, and what is heard comes by the preaching of Christ" (Romans 10:17).

The preacher will spend a lifetime learning to preach and may still feel like a beginner. Preaching is at once the greatest of challenges and the most wonderful of privileges.

✢　✢　✢　✢　✢

☞ Do you enjoy preaching? Is it something you look forward to?

☞ How well do you feel you preach?

☞ Is there a way to get someone to work with you so that your preaching might be improved?

# Ten

# Finding Sermon Topics

"Kent, what are you going to preach on tomorrow?" asked the voice on the other end of the line. (It was late on a Saturday night.)

"I am going through the Gospel of Mark and tomorrow I am working on chapter 4. How about you?"

"I haven't got anything at all."

"What is your favorite parable?" I asked.

"The one about the pearl of great price."

"Well, you might try that one." I thought I had solved the problem.

"I would, but I preached on it a couple weeks ago."

My friend and colleague faced a familiar dilemma, one that most preachers experience from time to time. And it is not a good place to be. This chapter is an attempt to minimize the agony of having little or nothing to preach on.

✤　　✤　　✤　　✤　　✤

Performance anxiety is something preachers must cope with their entire ministry, and without good sermon topics that anxiety can be greatly exacerbated. I am ill at ease, uncomfortable, anxious, and sometimes agitated when I am not confident about my sermon. It is better for me if I know what I will preach on weeks in advance. Not that the polished sermon must be ready, but at least I have the general topic and text.

Once in a while I simply have nothing to preach or at least nothing that I am excited about. What does a preacher do then? One option is to ask someone else to preach. Of course, this is rarely a viable alternative, especially in the smaller church. Preaching is more than throwing something together and that is what someone might be forced to do on short notice. I have asked someone to give his or her testimony; this is more realistic than expecting a sermon. If there is no other way, I will find a passage of Scripture I am familiar with, maybe a parable, a passage from Paul or a story from one of the Gospels. I will do little more than expose the passage. The congregation then will, at any rate, hear the Word of God.

Sermon ideas often come to me during my devotional reading. For the past several years all I have to do is read a Spurgeon or Nettleton sermon and I come across the beginnings of a sermon. Simply riding along in the car, sitting in the back yard, or talking with a friend is enough stimulation, somehow, for a sermon to take root in my mind. It is not uncommon for a member of the congregation to suggest a topic that appeals to me. There have been a few times when I have specifically asked the congregation to suggest sermon topics that interest them.

A series of sermons on The Lord's Prayer, the Beatitudes or the 23rd Psalm are generally well accepted. As a preacher, I may not personally be excited about a particular subject; it is enough to know that the congregation will benefit. However, most of the series sermons I have done over the years have worked out well. Recently I preached through the Apostles' Creed and loved every sermon. I have gone through the 23rd Psalm section by section, other times I have preached on favorite proverbs and parables. A series of profiles of major biblical characters is usually well received. Several times I have done a series on the sayings of Jesus, five or more of the better known ones. The same can be done with Paul. A series that I hope to do is on the letters to the seven churches of Asia in the Book of Revelation. Short books in the New Testament, Galatians, Ephesians, Philippians, Colossians, First and Second Timothy, First and Second Peter, First John, or Titus lend themselves to a series of sermons.

Some of the sermons of the great preachers of the past can be preached, read even, with very little alteration. Charles Hadden Spurgeon's sermons are especially useful. Not long ago I simply read a Spurgeon sermon. I have done the same thing with Asahel Nettleton, the great preacher of the first half of the Second Great Awakening. Nettleton's sermons need only slight alteration and they will preach perfectly today. In addition there are many such preachers who gladly lend their services. Anyone may use my paraphrase the Jonathan Dickinson sermon titled "The Theology of New Birth", that is included in this book under the chapter title "A Sermon to Have Ready to Preach". Right now I am preparing a three sermon series on a paper written by J.C. Ryle, an Anglican bishop of the Nineteenth Century, titled "The Fallibility of Ministers." (see J.C. Ryle's book, *Churches Beware!*, Evangelical Press, 1998)

To some degree I will follow the church calendar and preach on the traditional topics. During Advent for example, I will preach on various themes appropriate to the season. The same for the Easter season. About every other year I will speak on the major

Jewish feasts and festivals thereby giving me an opportunity to highlight our Christian roots.

It is said that the great Spurgeon did not think of or work on his sermon during the week; he wrote his sermon Saturday evening. I have questioned this, but Bob and Mike Ross of Pilgrim's Publications of Pasadena, Texas, reliable authorities on Spurgeon, verified Spurgeon's practice. I have seen samples of Spurgeon's sermon notes and that is all he prepared, notes. The sermons would be written out, often by other people, later on. He had an extraordinary gift. I can not do that; I have to be ahead a couple of weeks.

If I hear someone preach a good sermon I do not mind using it, giving credit where that is due.

It may be that I will sense a need the congregation has and prepare sermons designed to meet that need.

From time to time I have preached sermons a second time, that is, preached from the same outline. Generally I do not like to do this; more often I will develop a new outline. (I keep my sermons; they are categorized according to topic.)

The weekly pressure to come up with a sermon topic will be felt by preachers. There may be weeks when there is a flat, uninspired nature to the sermons. It is not our inspiration, certainly, that we are hoping to have, it is the inspiration of the Holy Spirit. This is the reason why a sermon should be anchored in the Scripture. A strong text and plenty of it will prove to be the best.

Some Sunday mornings when I have been sick, felt ill at ease or thought I had preached terribly—those sermons accomplished, seemingly, the most good. God will use for His glory and purpose that which we might not value. We preach "in season and out of season," prepare as best we can, and leave the results to the Holy Spirit.

In conclusion, let me briefly address one of the great debates about preaching: should sermons be expository only or are topical sermons acceptable as well. By expository I mean having a text of Scripture, a word, a phrase, a verse, a paragraph, maybe even a whole book, and then preaching on the meaning of the text, 'exposing' it, and finding applications for the converted and unconverted that arise naturally out of the text. Spurgeon was a master of this preaching.

This is the type of preaching strongly advocated by one of my favorite preachers, D. Martyn Lloyd-Jones. Many preachers would agree with Lloyd-Jones and believe that a topical sermon, speaking on a subject, is not good preaching.

I do not share that view. It seems that the sermons in Acts, those of Peter, Stephen, and Paul, are generally topical sermons. They are certainly biblical and that is the great criteria, the sermon must be biblical. The reason many of the great preachers warn against topical sermons is that there is a tendency for preachers to present their own ideas and notions rather than preach the Word of God. The people in the pews want "to see Jesus" and be instructed from the Scripture rather than hearing the preacher's thoughts.

I know from my own preaching why some of the great preachers advocate expository sermons so strongly. I admit I have often wanted to preach on a subject, could not easily find a verse that spoke directly to it and either simply picked a text that had something to do with the subject or preached without a text at all.

My rule is this: Be honest with a text. Get out of it what it says and do not add to it. If there is a compelling subject and no immediate text for it but you feel it is biblical, state the circumstance and preach the topical sermon.

Now it is perfectly proper to develop a topical sermon out of a biblical text. It is very common, and it is, of course, best if the points come right out of the text itself, usually by way of applying the text to people's lives.

Preachers must experiment, try this and that. Most congregations can take some of that. A particular style and approach to preaching will gradually develop. And however experienced we might be, we never quit studying the dynamics of preaching.

Often preachers start with a "skeleton", an idea and little else, and then later it is fleshed out. Sometimes however, they get "cold" and have to be thrown out.

☞ Is there anything in this or the last chapter that suggests a skeleton to you?

Eleven

# On Teaching the Bible

"You take the Bible too seriously," she said, "There are lots of other holy books but you never mention them."

She was right and I told her so. "When you love the Lord you will love His Word, too. Then you will like it that I preach the Bible."

"Never!" came the response and she hung up the phone.

✢    ✢    ✢    ✢    ✢

My conviction is that the Bible is the inspired Word of God. People wrote the Bible, yet in a way we do not understand, it is God's own Word. From Genesis to Revelation it has been "breathed" by the Holy Spirit. The Scripture is therefore reliable and without error; I can trust what the Bible says.

Views of the Bible range everywhere from, "It is not the word of God, simply the word of man," all the way to the "mechanistic" view, which essentially holds that the Bible was transmitted by God writing through human hands much like automatic writing in occult practices. Certainly there are many views that would fall in-between the extremes. My tendency is to avoid the controversies; I generally, though not always, stand clear of the "Bible battles".

The Holy Spirit must reveal, even apply Scripture in any case. Unconverted people will neither love nor appreciate the Word of God. The natural or unconverted person does not understand the things of the Spirit of God. (see 1 Corinthians 1:18, 2:14)

Christianized people, those, who have experienced false conversion, will be ambivalent toward the Bible at best and will have trouble understanding it. The Christianized can have an intellectual knowledge of the Bible, but will not come to love and cherish it. The Bible is a Holy Spirit book about Jesus, and only the Holy Spirit can make it understandable.

Pastors teach the Bible. This is the chief mechanism by which the Apostles' doctrine is communicated to the Church. (see Acts 2:42)

How is the Bible taught? One answer is: it must be taught in context. This is more complicated and important than it might first appear, and I am going to present, though briefly, one reason why the Bible's context must be clearly defined.

We must see that the cultural and religious context  of both the Old and New Testaments is Jewish. Philosophers reference two fundamentally distinct mindsets or ways of thinking about the world— a *Jewish, Hebrew or eastern* mindset and the w*estern* mindset. These are two differing ways of approaching almost everything, and this is particularly important when it comes to the Bible.

The *Jewish* or *Hebrew mindset* understands, for instance, that to say "in the name of Jesus" is to be making reference to the *person and work of Jesus* in totality including His deity and humanness, His death on the cross, His burial, His resurrection, and His ascension. When the Christian says, "in the name of Jesus" this is what should be meant. This is the *Hebrew mindset.*

In contrast, the w*estern mindset* would take "in the name of Jesus" in a much more literal fashion that almost approaches a magical way of thinking. The phrase is thought to have power in itself, in its very utterance. If the phrase is not pronounced at the end of a prayer, for example, the prayer would be considered ineffectual—this is a "western" view of prayer. The w*estern mindset*, that more literal approach to the Scripture, has been popular only for the last couple of hundred years. But it has almost become normative in many branches of evangelical Christianity.

In order to adequately teach the Bible then it must be put in its Jewish context. It is helpful, additionally, for the teacher of the Bible to understand the life and times of the Bible writers. There are many other points on teaching the Bible that can not be made in this short chapter.

The learning of and teaching of the Bible is a lifelong enterprise. If a pastor does not read the biblical languages, Hebrew and Greek, other tools can be used to compensate. A good concordance—an exhaustive concordance—is essential. A Bible atlas will find good use. I think it is important to have an interlinear Bible, both the Hebrew-English Old Testament and the Greek-English New Testament. I have known pastors to gradually pick up a considerable command of the biblical languages using interlinear Bibles. Bible dictionaries are very useful. Commentaries of the Bible as a whole and of individual books, especially those that incorporate analysis of the languages, can be obtained. I do not accept commentary as truth certainly. On occasion, I have consulted many commentaries on an issue and never agreed with a one. But they can be instructive even if they only serve to clarify what it is that must be rejected.

More and more I like to consult Spurgeon on a passage of Scripture. If a pastor is blessed to have Spurgeon's sermons, indexes will locate what Spurgeon said about many texts.

Bible study tools are fairly expensive. I imagine if I had to replace essential study tools I now have the cost would be around $2000, not an insignificant sum but a worthwhile investment.

I spend nearly as much time preparing for a Bible study with three or four people as I will for the Sunday morning service. I must admit that I am the one who benefits most. Preparation for Bible teaching and preaching is a most valuable and profitable time. Study of Scripture is what I love second most about the pastoral ministry.

My preference is to teach the Bible verse-by-verse. I am not particularly concerned with covering a certain amount of material. One verse may supply enough for an entire study; sometimes a whole chapter may be covered. But more than likely a paragraph or two will be gone over in any case.

In the Bible studies I teach I do not make an effort to be entertaining, I merely seek to expose the Scripture. The truth of the Bible is enough; it is not necessary for me to be exciting. Of course, it is no virtue to be boring.

The Scripture must be dealt with as it really is. Some parts of it are difficult to understand. The Bible teacher must be able to admit when a particular passage is difficult, even obscure. Any teacher of the Word who has been at it for a time will adopt a humble approach to the Bible. One of the most annoying tendencies of a teacher is the intimation of extraordinary knowledge of the Scripture. Being willing to admit to a lack of understanding of a passage or concept or saying is becoming of the Bible teacher. Often I will present contrary views on a passage and even seem, for didactic reasons, to champion them.

It is the Holy Spirit who must impress the truth upon any hearer. The teacher, then, relies upon God's Spirit to be the real teacher though every effort is made to handle the Word of God appropriately and honestly.

Teaching the Bible from the pulpit is a favorite form of preaching because the gospel is on every page. My preaching is sometimes very much like teaching though I believe the two are different. Teaching is exposing the Scripture, preaching is applying it to the converted and unconverted. Teaching from Scripture becomes a sermon when the truth of it is applied to the hearers. At Miller Avenue we have a "Bible Exposition," which is verse by verse teaching of the Scripture. Then a hymn is sung before the sermon is presented.

I do not consider myself to be much of a preacher though I strive to be the best preacher I can be. Preaching and teaching go together, both are essential. I think it is accurate to say that I have placed my emphasis on teaching. My feeling is that if I can communicate the Scripture then I am moving along toward fulfilling my pastoral responsibilities.

✢    ✢    ✢    ✢    ✢

☞ Do you see a difference between teaching and preaching?

☞ How do you see yourself in terms of strengths and weaknesses?

☞ Do you take any pleasure in teaching the Scripture?

# Twelve

# Discussion of the Sermon

I felt like I had been kicked in the stomach. "Why do you insist on shouting at us like we were children?" he asked in something less than a pleasant tone of voice. "Not only that, I didn't appreciate your reference to the Catholic Church."

The fact is I had invited this kind of feedback.

After a sermon I am sometimes worn out and need time to recover, and an attack on my person and my sermon both was tough to take. "Those are good points," I began, "Let me try to explain myself." And so I did and I think he accepted what I said though he might not have agreed completely. He did keep coming and attends to this day. It was better for him to voice his complaints than have them drive him away.

✢　✢　✢　✢　✢

A preacher ought to be accountable for what is presented in the sermon. As a way of making that happen, after the service at Miller Avenue, everyone is invited to stay for "coffee hour" and a discussion of the sermon. We have coffee, tea, cookies, and sometimes, a light lunch. There are some old couches and a coffee table in one particular section of our fellowship hall where we gather to eat and discuss the sermon.

People will often have questions and comments after hearing a sermon. There have been affirmations and confirmations, there have also been some anger expressed. Everything is welcome and the sessions can even be quite helpful to the preacher as well as to others. Some important work is accomplished during the discussion of the sermon.

There are some alert, sophisticated people at Miller Avenue who are not afraid to be critical and will challenge me. I, of course, am very aware of this, and try to be careful not to put myself into a bad situation; I have learned to be careful about the things that I say. Ministerial exaggerations, mean spiritedness, attacking people and/or institutions, these will not go unnoticed or unmentioned. I am not above defending myself and I will not back down from preaching the truth either, but I know I will be held accountable when I go where I should not.

There is a helpful saying, "We agree to disagree". I am not looking for uniformity in doctrine, or expecting people to use words and phrases that I use. We are not all at the same place theologically or spiritually, and room must be made for differences. Debate and discussion is characteristic of maturity, and so is becoming accountable for the content of the sermon. Accountability can actually result in better preaching.

✢　✢　✢　✢　✢

 Have you ever wanted to talk with a preacher about a sermon?

 I assume the answer is yes. Some people may want to do the same with your sermons. Could you handle it?

# Thirteen

# Listening to Criticism

"Did you hear yourself? You're being overly critical, Kent."

"Critical, I'm not a critical person."

"Ha, so you think. I've been married to you so long and you think I don't know."

I've been told I tend to be a critical person. I don't like this about myself and I have to guard against it or I would alienate everyone around me. And as a pastor it would be deadly if I did not check it. At the same time I don't like to be criticized. Perhaps my fear of criticism is related to my tendency to criticize others.

✣　✣　✣　✣　✣

Early on in my Christian life, there were a few things about the church I attended that I would have loved to have talked over with my pastor. The concerns were not of great significance. More than anything else, I only wanted to spend time with the pastor. Making a suggestion or critique is one way of coming before the pastor.

Criticisms tend to be presented shortly before the Sunday morning worship service is to begin. The next best time is actually during the worship service itself, even right before the sermon, via a note or a whisper. Many criticisms come immediately after the service. It is rare for someone to make an appointment for lunch, coffee, or a chat in the office and express a critique in a way that is intended to be encouraging and helpful.

Pastors are frequently admonished, mainly through denominational publications, "Listen to criticism and evaluate it". And pastors might more often do so if they recognized a criticism for what it was. But the so-called criticism may seem like a personal attack, and it may be just that, a personal attack.

Here is a list of some of the ordinary criticisms.

1. You are not talking loud enough when you preach, or, you are talking too loud when you preach.

2. You are not using the Bible enough in your sermons, or, you are using the Bible too much in your sermons.

3. Your sermons are too long, or, your sermons are too short.

4. You sing too many hymns in the service, or, you do not sing enough hymns in the service.

5. There is not enough praying in the service, or, you are praying too much in the service.

6. The services last too long, or, the services are too short.

7. I wish the Holy Spirit would be present in the service.

8. The services are becoming awfully lively are they not?

9. We are having far too many guest speakers, or, why don't we have more guest speakers?

10. I wish you would speak so that the children could understand you, or, I wish you would speak more to the adults and mature Christians in the congregation.

11. I wish you would preach the gospel more, or, Why are you always preaching to the unconverted?

12. When are we going to get some new families into the church?

There may be no way to make sense out of a criticism and perhaps the best one can do is hear the criticism, thank the person, and make an expression that it will be considered and prayed about. Or, if is of a very serious nature, the pastor can state that others will be consulted. A last resort response is to state that the issue will be brought up before the church council.

There is a difference between a suggestion and a criticism. Everyone will have a suggestion from time to time. Anyone who cares about their church will make suggestions. It seems that I can feel the difference between a suggestion and a criticism. The person who makes a suggestion is often willing to volunteer to make the suggestion a reality. A suggestion does not call into question the spirituality, dedication, motive, vision, faithfulness, and integrity of the pastor. Words like "why" and "how come" are not used, and no comparisons are made.

A person who talks about how things were in their old church is not making, necessarily, a criticism, and may not be making a suggestion either. They had appreciated and valued the ministry they received in a previous church and want to have the same kind of ministry in their new church if possible. I have learned much from people bringing new ideas to me; however, it is a rare situation where something that worked in one church will work in another. A sincere person whose suggestions spring from previous church experiences should be seriously considered, but I have learned not to make promises. If a suggestion comes that I find interesting, I will take it under consideration, talk with others about it, and even submit it to the church council.

When I was much younger I had a more difficult time accepting suggestions. I was far surer of myself when I was in my 30s and 40s, and now as I find myself in my late 50s, I am much more open to change. I am not sure why; I think it is because I realize that as long as I get to preach the gospel I do not much care what else happens. Therefore I am probably more open to suggestion and critique than at any other time in my life.

Many suggestions, and criticisms, have to do with the content and structure of the worship service. The long and short of it is there is only so much that can be done in a worship service unless no time limit is put on it. The worship service almost becomes a war zone in some churches. When pressed I have simply replied: "How about you creating the worship services for the next month?" And I have done it, actually let the suggestion makers and critics design the service. Then I have had the opportunity to use that old line, "If it is too hot, get out of the kitchen"

There will be people who seem to be making a critique, but actually they are making an evaluation of the pastor and the pastoral ministry. It is a disguised attack. It may come from jealousy; it may come from envy. It may be that the person covets the pastor's position. They may see themselves in a leadership position, and they may be, even at an unconscious level, wanting to diminish the pastoral authority that theirs might be elevated. The worst response is a refusal to listen to or consider the suggestion/critique.

Pastors must understand that they do not have it all figured out, and, of course, just because somebody makes a suggestion does not mean it must be accepted as valid and acted upon. In the best of times I like to be able to say, "Thank you for saying that. I am going to take that under consideration. I am going to talk to some other people about that, and let us talk about it in month or so."

On a few occasions I have asked suggestion makers to put their ideas down on paper that I might study it and perhaps use it to make a presentation to the church council. Now accountability is built into the process. Many a suggestion has withered on the vine when people must stand behind their suggestion. After a time, when such a process is used and becomes well know to others, the number of suggestions may be radically reduced.

There are probably a couple of dozen other ways of dealing with suggestions and criticisms. There are times when the last thing a pastor needs is to discover that someone else in the congregation has a critique or evaluation. However, listening to these goes with the territory of being a pastor. Suggestions and criticisms must be heard and evaluated.

Reflect for a moment to recall how it is that you react to suggestions and criticisms.

☞ If your reflection reveals you do not like suggestions and criticisms, is there room for personal growth? If you are like me, this is not easily done.

Fourteen

# Public Ministry—Is it a Performance?

"I love being in front of people. That's what I miss most."

My friend was telling the truth. He had, in fact, majored in theater while in college. Out of politeness, however, I decided not to challenge his statement. It bothered me though; we pastors are hypocritical enough without making the worship service a performance.

✟   ✟   ✟   ✟   ✟

By public ministry I mean any service or meeting where there is some kind of presentation to people—a worship service, an organizational meeting, a workshop, even a Bible study.

Unwittingly I started out in the pastoral ministry thinking like a performer—I tried to preach like Billy Graham. I thought I would be successful if I copied the greatest preacher of the Twentieth Century. During my first pastorate I mimicked Graham to the point people commented on it, and I would be flattered. If great crowds of people had packed in to hear me, I probably would still be sounding like I was from North Carolina.

Some years later, during the Jesus People Movement, someone suggested I preach like Oral Roberts. I tried but I failed; I could do Graham better than Roberts. After many years I finally let the stylized preaching go and allowed the natural Philpott to emerge. But the temptation to emulate the great preachers is strong.

In conversations with other ministers about this particular situation, I have come to the conclusion there is almost an addictive kind of allure to public ministry. To stand before others and receive their acclamation, appreciation, admiration, attention, and respect is a heady phenomenon, so much so that it can become a primary motive for ministry. An extreme illustration of the power of being before others is the preacher who gauged his success on how many standing ovations he received during the course of a sermon.

For many years I was in public ministry and then for a space of several years I was not. I confess I missed standing before a group of people and receiving their attention. My flesh, to use Pauline terms, seemed to revel in and hunger for the "spotlight". Often, too often, my fleshly craving for the applause of people spurred me on. Not that God can not use this, if it is submitted to Christ, but it is a craving, a potentially addictive thing, that can eventually bring harm.

Certainly, the alternative, a fear of being in front of people, is also damaging. I remember being anxious, very anxious sometimes, and occasionally I still am. If I speak before a group I am not familiar with I may have considerable anxiety. Even at Miller Avenue I occasionally will begin to be anxious Saturday night or on Sunday morning. If I am not confident in my preparation or discover that I no longer like the sermon, my anxiety level will go up. When I feel I have a good handle on the sermon and am looking forward to preaching it, there is little if any anxiety. When I know that unconverted people will be present I am often looking forward to preaching.

There is another kind of anxiety, however, that I often experience, that has nothing to do with standing before a group of people. Perhaps "anxiety" is not the right word. What I feel is a kind of inadequacy. I will doubt my ability to communicate Jesus and His wonderful love. As a sinner myself, I stand before others with the task of preaching the gospel. It comes to me as I imagine it must have to Paul, I am in fear and trembling. And this has nothing to do with stage fright. I am fearful that I might not do my job as a preacher in a way that would please and honor God. At little stage fright is nothing in comparison.

But there is a danger that public ministry might devolve into a performance; the preacher or teacher becomes an actor. My feeling is, although I have no statistics on this and few concrete illustrations that I would relate here, a ministry would eventually be undermined under such circumstances. A congregation will begin to sense they are witnessing a performance. Pastors should not underestimate the acuity and wisdom of the people they preach to. If a pastor has an ego that needs to be continually fed, the unction of the Holy Spirit will be thwarted and people may disregard the message however biblical.

Pastors conduct their ministries because of their relationship with Jesus Christ, the motive being to honor and serve our Lord, and to lift up His name. As Spurgeon said, "The audience is not in the pews, it is in heaven."

✣  ✣  ✣  ✣  ✣

☞ Fear of speaking before a group of people—have you experienced this?

☞ Have you developed your own style of preaching?

☞ Do you relate to the "performance" idea presented in this chapter?

## Fifteen

# Keeping Strong and Healthy

"I figured God would take care of me. I never thought I had to take care of myself."

So spoke a pastor friend while recuperating at home following a heart attack that almost killed him. Forty pounds overweight, a sedentary life style, and lots of stress had nearly finished off this forty-one year old former athlete.

✤　✤　✤　✤　✤

The ministry is a physically demanding job. A pastor has to be strong and healthy to be able to preach, teach, and fulfill the never-ending responsibilities.

The problem is, much of the time a pastor is either sitting or standing—not moving; it is not necessarily all office work, but a great deal of it is. Therefore, steps need to be taken to maintain, if not build up, strength and health.

At minister's meetings there will often be considerable discussion of body weight, diet, blood pressure, cholesterol counts, and other health and medical topics. Many of the meetings involve a meal, usually a lunch; ministers "do" lots of breakfast and lunch meetings. Too many ministers seem to be lumpy, pasty, flabby, and out of shape.

Personally I go to a gym and workout three days a week. It is not always possible for me to maintain that schedule. For example, today I will not make it to the gym so that I can work on this book. But I am going to get in two good days this week no matter what. I begin with a run on a treadmill then I get on a stationary bicycle; I get in at least 20 minutes of aerobic exercise. Next comes stretching. Then I lift weights, which is my favorite part. At the time of this writing I am 58 years old, and I can still bench press 205 pounds (tops is 225), and I can do more pull-ups and chin-ups than most people.

Notice I called what I do at the gym a "work-out". It is work and there is always some pain and discomfort associated with the exercises. Stretching is my least favorite activity, but I do it so I will be able to tie my shoes when I am a hundred years old.

Exercise and fitness have been a priority with me for 20 years. It allows me to be strong enough to be one of the baseball coaches at San Quentin Prison. This last weekend I played 18 innings of baseball, actually nine innings of baseball on Saturday at the prison and nine innings of softball on Sunday against the local Catholic Church. A few times I had to run the bases, and I was okay after that. I attribute this to a consistent workout program. When I go to the doctor for my annual physical I hear "Whatever you're doing keep doing it".

If I can do this anyone can. I strongly encourage pastors to commit to a regular exercise program. Find what it is that works best in terms of exercises and do not give up. It might be a workout consisting of swimming, fast walking, bicycling, running, jogging, and so forth. Remember it is a "work-out," it is WORK and not necessarily pleasure. And, it takes all the discipline I've got.

Certainly it is important to eat right. Truth is I eat what I want, but I watch what and how much. I have a tendency to put on weight; I used to weigh 20 more pounds than I do now. It was very difficult for me to take weight off even with a rigorous exercise program. I found that if I eliminate a meal now and then, and it is usually lunch, that helps me.

I suggest being involved in or at least interested in some kind of sport. I take a great interest in baseball— I am a San Francisco Giants fan, and currently I am a coach of the San Quentin Prison's Giants Baseball Club (my fourth year). Also I am very interested in professional football—a San Francisco 49er fan. And, of course, I follow the Oakland Raiders, the Oakland Athletics, and Golden State Warriors. I play golf rarely, but I continue to play tennis and surf with bogey boards at the beach.

The preaching of the gospel is more stressful and requires more energy than most people imagine. To stand up and preach a good solid gospel sermon for 45 to 60 minutes is not a task easily undertaken. Nothing tires me out so much as preaching. It takes more out of me to preach than to play baseball. We need to keep strong and healthy in order to preach the gospel.

Lastly, the example set by the pastor in terms of fitness and diet will help members of the congregation. "If the pastor does it, it must be worth doing" will run through the minds of many. Paul told Timothy that exercise or physical training is of "some value". (see 1 Timothy 4:8) Godliness is of greater value certainly, yet physical training does have "some value". God willing, keeping fit may add years of additional service we might not otherwise enjoy.

☞ What is the state of your health?

☞ Do you have an exercise program?

☞ Do you eat healthy foods?

☞ Do you think any of this matters?

Sixteen

# Early to Bed, Early to Rise...

"You can't soar with the eagles in the morning if you are hooting with the owls at night." I don't know if Prince Altom, pastor of Hillside Church of Marin, made this up or not, but they were certainly words I needed to hear.

✢　　✢　　✢　　✢　　✢

My habit is to rise about 7AM, drink a cup or two of coffee while I read the newspaper, eat a substantial breakfast, and then leave for the office.

I find I do my best work in the morning. Once in my office, Bible reading, prayer, and reflection come first. Secondly, I focus on the sermon. Last of all I briefly study one language or another.

It is best if this time is without interruption. When the phone starts ringing the day is on (there is no secretary at Miller Avenue). Other activities, appointments, correspondence, computer work, and so on, begin around 10AM.

In order to rise early I must retire early as well. Part of keeping strong and healthy is getting plenty of sleep. A lack of sleep over the course of a few days means the body and brain are not going to work as they could.

Good nutrition is important, but it will not make up for a lack of sleep and/or a weak body. A pastor is similar to an athlete who must keep in training all the time. To compete the athlete must eat right, get good sleep, and exercise regularly. All Christians are in a race, a competition, and it is the wise and prudent pastor who runs hard toward the prize.

Having said all this I want to say that this regime, that suits me, may not suit everyone. Several pastors I know work the opposite from me, that is, they do their best work at night, sometimes quite late at night, and consequently they sleep late into the next day. We are all different and every one of us will find what works best for them.

☞ The pastor as athlete—does this seem to be an apt comparison?

☞ What about your lifestyle, does it contribute to health and strength?

Seventeen

# The Pastor's Work Schedule

"I punched the time clock in and out every day for twenty years. Now though I come to the office at the church and it is just me. There is no one around all day long. How do you get anything done?"

✢　✢　✢　✢　✢

Most pastors have heard the little joke; "We pay you for working an hour a week." I used to laugh at it but now I don't.

Pastoral ministry is unusual in many ways; certainly it is unlike any other job I've had. People used to working 9-5 may have a difficult time adjusting to the work schedule typical of the pastoral ministry. They may have a difficult time realizing they are working when they are simply reading the Scripture, studying for a sermon, or reflecting on some theological point. I have known more than one person who could not adjust. The fact is, it has taken me most of my life to feel comfortable with the lifestyle of the pastoral ministry.

Additionally, pastoral ministry will be difficult for those who are unable to motivate themselves and schedule their own time. The work is open-ended without clear beginning and ending points. It is often the case that there is no one to observe, much less monitor, the progress or pace of the workday. This is especially true for the small church pastor.

To cope with the peculiarities of the ministry I created a schedule for myself. I try to get an early start. Scripture reading and prayer come first. Sermon and Bible study preparation follow. Then, as I am my own secretary, I deal with correspondence and e-mail, and make and return phone calls. Generally this work is accomplished by noon. Some days this actually happens. However, if I am too anxious about fulfilling a schedule, I will become frustrated and irritable. The pastoral ministry is unpredictable and allowances for the unexpected must be made.

Pastors can find themselves working seven days a week, ten to twelve hours each day, if they are not careful. Therefore, I encourage pastors to observe a Sabbath rest. If Sunday is able to be the actual Sabbath rest despite the worship and preaching, teaching, and other ministry, well, that's fine. But it may be necessary to find another day. It is vitally important to rest from our labors as the Scripture teaches.

I have found that it helps to break the workday down into three segments: morning, afternoon, and evening. If I am not careful, I will work morning, afternoon, and evening. Much of pastoral ministry goes on in the evening so unless time is taken off during the day, a morning or afternoon, a pastor will end up working way more than is healthy. After a while, weeks or months maybe, exhaustion will set in. It is not unusual for a pastor to work 70 to 90 hours a week without realizing it.

If I'm working in the morning (and I always work in the morning), and I'm going to be working in the evening, I'll want to be able to rest some in the afternoon. If I have nothing in the evening, then I'll work in the afternoon. But I try to avoid working all three segments of the day. This is an ideal anyway. I admit to working six days a week; I am rarely able to take a complete day off. Things happen in the ministry; people and their problems can not be easily put off.

Vacations are generally a problem for me. First there is the preparation required in order to leave, and then there is the tremendous amount of catch-up upon the return. Some vacations have produced more work than work itself. Despite the problems it is important to get away from time to time.

Short trips, a day or two in duration, seem to work well for me. These are more easily managed and financed, and they require less preparation and catch-up. My kids need the week or two away on vacation though; the longer vacations are more for my girls than for my wife and I.

The pastoral ministry has some resemblance to artistic pursuits. The musician, the artist, the poet, the novelist—these require time for reflection, time for free-form thinking. I have a custom of sitting at night, usually outside in good weather, thinking over the past day and thinking through what is coming up the next. I clear out the old day and get ready for the new day. From Scripture I have learned to let the "evil" for the day be sufficient for that day. It is taking one day at a time, praying that God will give me the "bread" for the coming day and thanking Him for the provision for the past day. I try not to worry overmuch about the day coming up until I get to it. When tomorrow arrives, I'll let yesterday go. It's like the baseball player who forgets about the last at bat and focuses instead on the one coming up. Whether the result was a strike out or a home run it doesn't make any difference, the process is the same—forget about the last one; focus on the next one.

People unacquainted with the pastoral ministry might not appreciate the lifestyle. Furthermore, pastors should not compare themselves to those who are perhaps fortunate enough to have a regularly scheduled work routine.

People may not realize that teaching a one-hour Bible study may involve hours of preparation. In addition, the work is not necessarily over when the Bible study or prayer meeting is concluded. Sometimes, when the meeting is officially over, the real work is just beginning. And few see this. Then again, it is not so easy, after engaging in serious ministry with people well into the night, to be able to go home and fall right to sleep; there is wind-down time. The pastoral ministry demands a whole different approach to work. A pastor must be sensitive to that and not be apologetic for it either.

Someone might reason, "You're not doing anything, you're not active, you're not running around, you're not physically producing something." Regardless of the misunderstandings, going for a walk to think about things, taking a drive, going to a park, sitting by a stream—these times can be very important. We don't have to always be engaged in concrete action. It is, in fact, important to sit and look and listen.

Consider the various work schedules you have had.

☞ How is the pastoral ministry different?

☞ Are you a self-motivator?

☞ Do you feel comfortable working alone?

# Eighteen

# Personal Finances and Life-style

"I've spent ten years in graduate schools and I make less money than the guy working down at the 7-11 store. And I am tired of it. I've got to figure a way to make more money and if I can't here at the church, well, I guess I might have to leave. This simply can not continue."

Who was this pastor? Me!

✤　✤　✤　✤　✤

Very few pastors accumulate any considerable amount of wealth. How much is enough and how much is too much is debatable. Rarely do pastors earn the equivalent of what someone in another field with the same abilities, education, and experience would earn. This is perhaps a good thing.

Pastors, I believe, must learn how to live a simple life. For example, it is extremely important to avoid debt. I think a sound principle is "If there is not enough cash to buy it, don't buy it."

Situations may arise where the use of a credit card is necessary, perhaps in the purchase of a car or to cover major medical or dental costs. But living a simple life style and being content with it will free a pastor from much stress and anxiety.

One of the sins that pastors are sometimes tempted with is covetousness. Ministers of large churches whose salaries may be more than adequate, who may either own their own homes or be in the process of buying one, who may take expensive long vacations, who may be granted periodic sabbaticals, and who may be off doing other wonderful things—these may tempt a less financially advantaged pastor to covetousness with a little envy thrown in as well. In addition the large church minister may have a great health plan and a lot of money in a pension fund. For a pastor to be financially well off is not wrong, but it is somewhat unique and beyond reality for most.

"Middle class" is an apt description of my life style, thus, I consider myself to be quite well off. (I could live on less.) My income must provide for a family of four, my wife and I and our two children. I have to have money to operate the household, keep the cars on the road, the IRS happy, and the insurance companies paid. Therefore it is required that I do this in the best way possible and I do it with what the church can provide combined with what my wife and I earn in other ways. It seems to me that we Philpotts enjoy our lives and have the necessities met. I have never had a situation of extreme need. There have been difficult times, but God has provided for us all the way along.

Pastors should be careful to tithe all income and provide for offerings beyond the tithe. Giving is best when it is done on a "cheerful" basis with gratefulness for God's provision. All giving should be done in secret, not letting the "left hand know what the right hand is doing". Only the treasurer and/or bookkeeper would know the details. Pastors do not want to be talking about their patterns of giving.

I have not taken a salary increase the entire time I have been at Miller Avenue. Now, I want to be careful to say that in a way that does not sound boastful. The truth is, I have taken certain perks over the years—benefit increases here and there. But I keep it to a minimum. I do not like to continually come to the church asking for more money. Every year this small church has wanted to increase the salary of their pastor. And I have declined that, and with thanksgiving, too, that people would be concerned for me. My goal has been to prevent the church from getting into a situation where money was a problem. I know many churches like to have a continually increasing budget, and we do in a very small way, but I like to keep the church in the black. Running behind budget thus necessitating a situation where the congregation has to be continually appealed to is something I want to avoid almost at all costs.

It has been my custom to work outside the church. (I'm going to be talking in another chapter about having a trade.) At the outset of my pastoral ministry at Miller Avenue I asked for permission that I be free to engage in other means, in limited and appropriate ways, in order to increase my income if necessary. Currently, primarily through weddings and funerals, I do make some extra income. For several years my wife and I operated a part time legal service. The additional income has kept the financial pressure off the congregation.

Living a simple life and keeping finances pretty much on a cash basis has worked for me personally. Good churches want to see that their pastors are cared for and their needs met. And it is important that the pastor is not constantly presenting needs. Some refer to this as "whining". If there are some needs not being covered then those needs should be dealt with in a very careful way. Constantly presenting the church with needs can become discouraging to any group of people. A congregation may even feel guilty and may not know how to meet the needs.

If I were independently wealthy I might think about paying the church to be able to be the pastor and preach the gospel on Sunday morning. It is my chief joy to preach Jesus and I would be so very poor if I could not. Certainly, I could find other avenues for gospel preaching, but I love these people and this community and I want to pastor right here. Therefore, as best I can, I will do what it takes to be a gospel preacher and trust that God will meet my needs.

☞ How attached are you to credit cards?

☞ Do you panic when the money is low or nonexistent?

☞ Are you content with what you have?

## PASTOR'S BULLETIN BOARD

—Seeking counsel on a particular situation.

—Sharing programs you have found helpful.

—Needing an associate or assistant pastor.

—Looking for a church to pastor.

—Sermon outlines.

—Asking for prayer support.

—Other concerns.

Go to Earthenvessel.net and post it.

If you want to ask Philpott about any particular issue, feel free to do so.

Nineteen

# Deciding What Ministry to Engage In

"I've lived a block away from you for six years. Don't you ever get to know your neighbors?"

The truth is that in all these years I have rarely knocked on my neighbor's doors. Let me take that back, the first month or so on the job I did a little of that. I hated it; I would stand at the door and smile, introduce myself and hold out a brochure for people to take. And nothing ever came of it; not even one person ever came to church. I gave up on that.

✢    ✢    ✢    ✢    ✢

This is a far more complicated subject than can be adequately dealt with here. There are many wise and experienced people who have devoted lengthy volumes to this particular issue. I do not mean to do much more than talk about how Miller Avenue developed a few ministries.

In my mind, there is one ministry above all others and that is the preaching of the gospel so that people might come to Jesus for salvation. To have all the ministries conceivable and possible in operation yet not preach a strong conversion oriented gospel, in my view, is no ministry at all. Worse than that, it is deceptive and dangerous. If, with the ministry of the Word in place, and there is yet strength, time, and money for other ministries, very well.

Whether a new church is begun or a new pastor comes into an ongoing church, it is probably helpful that nothing be developed early on except the worship service, Bible study, and prayer meeting. Several years may be required before an adequate evaluation of a need for other services and ministries can be made. "Field Study" is a term for such an evaluation and many denominations will help local churches develop a ministry strategy.

It may take several years before a pastor can become familiar with a community in terms of the kinds of services and outreaches offered by other churches and social/political agencies. In addition, it takes time to assess the capabilities and gifts of a congregation on the one hand and the opportunities afforded and limitations mandated by a building, owned or rented, on the other. A careful evaluation is a time consuming process and not something to be rushed into.

Money is often a limiting factor; however, it is possible to develop significant outreaches and ministries with a small budget. Our Divorce Recovery Workshop program, for instance, which is in its fifteenth year, was started with $500.00, and it has paid for itself ever since. The television ministry is essentially cost free. (There is the possibility of sending videotapes of the program all over the country, but this would be costly and demand the creation of a major enterprise. My preference is to remain local and avoid the entanglements that would come with a large television ministry.) Our website cost us a few thousand dollars initially, yet we now maintain it with just twenty dollars a month. (There are now means of beginning a website for a fraction of what we spent.) Our Saturday lunch program required a couple of hundred dollars at first but it is virtually cost free now.

There is a need for a Sunday school at Miller Avenue. There are a lot of kids in our community who would benefit from our having a strong Sunday school. I would simply love to have one, but we have only an adult class at present.

We have a wonderful choir. In the congregation were people who were gifted musically so that it was a natural ministry to begin. Growing out of our small Sunday morning choir is an annual gospel concert, and we fill the place up. This is an outreach as well because people are attracted who would not otherwise be exposed to the gospel. The choir, especially the annual gospel concert, is a major effort for our small church and well worth everything we put into it.

I am attracted to a ministry that can involve a number of people and is the reason I like the San Quentin Prison ministry. The television program operates with two or three people. The Divorce Recovery Workshop again requires only a few people. But the choir can involve a large number of people, and the prison ministry is open ended, too. In addition, I am interested in a ministry that does not require a capital fund campaign to get it off the ground.

Ministries will occasionally fail and almost always there will be difficulties. This is understood going in. Not every ministry survives, very few survive for any length of time. Every ministry or outreach involves a certain amount of risk and a pastor must be a risk taker, in fact, the whole congregation must be willing to assume some risk. A church is not a business and can not be run on business principles though much is said to the contrary. Many things done at Miller Avenue are not cost effective. At this point, the website we maintain, for example, is not bringing in any money and so far, very few "hits." (Since I wrote that last sentence the website traffic has increased at least ten fold.) This is a ministry that requires patience and a vision for what it may be. The website may turn out to be a failure; we may abandon it one day. So what! Ministries will fail and when they do there will be something new to explore. Even if a particular program survives for only a short time, it is better to have made the attempt than to have done nothing at all. By way of illustration, it is a sad and unworthy baseball player who will quit after an unsuccessful season. Pastors and churches take risks. Assessments are made, plans developed, then "to the work," and the programs are continued for as long as possible.

People make mistakes in ministry; they will sometimes make rather large mistakes. Hopefully a program will have some checks and balances, but this is not always possible. Particularly I watch anything to do with children; it is necessary to be very careful with anything to do with children. Also, I take care to examine legal liabilities since we are in California and have to be aware that some people engage in insurance fraud and are quick to exploit any real or imagined injury.

When mistakes are made the pastoral response is critical. One lesson I've learned the hard way is to not immediately accept negative criticisms about any outreach. A fact finding process must sometimes be set in motion all the while conducted in a non-threatening, non-accusatory manner. A third, uninvolved person may be brought in to serve as a facilitator in a conflict resolution process. The goal is not always to continue the ministry, a larger goal may be to maintain fellowship and bring healing to any injury.

Newly converted people who are excited about serving Jesus may get involved in some ministry. Youthful zeal is a wonderful thing, but down the line the inexperienced person may get into some difficulty. Everything is not going to run smoothly. Pastoral response to trouble must be calming, reassuring, deliberate, fair, and reasonable. It may well be that the pastor must take responsibility and pick up the slack; pastors often pay the price for something that goes awry. The pastor, as shepherd, must protect the sheep from the wolf. Knowing which is which, however, is not always obvious.

The first church I pastored was in the heart of a vast agricultural area. A second year seminarian, I only had the weekends to be "in the field". For the two and one half years I was there our ministry consisted of two Sunday services. That is not completely correct either; after a while I shut down the Sunday evening service due to lack of interest—mine and everyone else's. Did I fail? No, I think not. I did what I could with what I had. Some people were converted, baptized, taught, and married. We prayed, sang, and worshipped the Lord. Those were good and wonderful years, years of fruitful ministry.

Let me emphasize one last point. I have a particular interest in engaging in a ministry for the long run. Ministry for the short run is questionable in my mind. By way of illustration we have engaged in these ministries: the Divorce Recovery Workshop—15 years, the television program—16 years, gospel choir—10 years, the ministry at San Quentin—fourteen years. We started the Saturday lunch four years ago. We are into our fourth year of the website ministry. If something is worth beginning, it is usually worth continuing, whether it seems to be successful right away or not.

Circumstances can change very quickly. Several years ago the Divorce Recovery Workshop went through a period where hardly anybody came. Some of our leaders quit and the money ran dangerously low. I determined to keep going and now, all of a sudden, it has grown some.

It is easy to work hard when there is obvious success. The real challenge comes when seeming failure looms. Now we are encouraged with the divorce recovery workshop, but we did not quit when things were going badly. I remember the very second workshop, only one person attended, and, all our leaders quit. People said, "Well, this won't work." But we kept it going. The workshop after that we had about five, and after that we had about twenty, and then twenty-five, and so it went. (At the time of this writing it has dipped again.) When a decision is made to begin a particular ministry, it should be given every chance of working. It may be years before any "fruit" appears.

As long as there is a motivated leader, a ministry may continue. That is the criteria: when there is no leader, the ministry is finished. But not before.

In your mind you may have ministries you hope to do. Make a list of them in order of importance to you personally.

☞ Is there a ministry you begun that failed?

☞ What happened then?

Twenty

# Church Structure

"I am absolutely meetinged out. Meetings, meetings, meetings! Is that all you do is have meetings?"

Would you, pastor, have to answer, "Yes"?

✤　✤　✤　✤　✤

E very church need not be run like Miller Avenue Baptist Church. Of course not! However, our structure forms the basic illustration for this chapter, because I think it is a workable structure for a small church.

The thesis for this chapter is: the church structure should be simple enough that distractions from the primary goal and mission of the church are minimized.

We have one single board, a church council, consisting of nine members. I am a permanent member of the church council. The other eight members serve for three years at a time and then must be off for one year. And they must be nominated and approved by the congregation. We meet once a month; we will skip a month now and again (usually in August and sometimes in December).

The church council functions as the church administrator, the clearing-house. The council does the "dirty work". Everything is on the basis of consensus; no vote is taken. Issues are debated until a resolution and/or consensus is reached.

We do have a budget committee that meets for about two hours a year to prepare the budget, which then goes to the church council, which then goes to the congregation.

There are four quarterly congregational meetings. At the third quarterly meeting the budget is presented. If and when it passes it means that the pastor and staff are hired for another year. Of course, I can be fired at any time, but generally it is understood that when the budget is passed the pastor's salary is approved. I can count on another year then unless something truly atrocious occurs. And it is always possible to be terminated and I'm going to address that issue in another chapter.

The simpler the structure the less time will be spent keeping it all in place. Once a number of committees have been established, the following will be "forever" coming up:

1. Attending committee meetings.
2. Replacing members who have fallen aside, moved, changed church membership, or whatever the reason.
3. Settling disputes between committee members.
4. Interpreting the decisions of the committees to the rest of the congregation.

The personal politics, the personal *petty* politics, involved in on-going committees and boards can be more than a pastor would ever want to be involved in. I simply have no committees.

In our constitution various committees are described and can be staffed if necessary. (A copy of our constitution can be emailed to you by request at either kentphilpott@home.com or earthenvessel.net.) If I were to be terminated, a pastoral search committee would have to be selected. On paper we have that committee, but it is not staffed. If we need a building committee to investigate repairs then that committee can be created. But to maintain committees can be, and usually is, an unpleasant and unnecessary experience!

Let me illustrate our church structure with our Saturday Lunch. The people who run it are the people who participate in it; they are the ones who actually do the work. Problems they encounter are worked out internally, and if this proves impossible, they are taken to the church council. Furthermore, there is no oversight committee for the Saturday Lunch, the Divorce Recovery Workshop, or the Parenting Workshop. There is no committee that oversees the San Quentin or television ministry. There is no oversight committee except the church council.

I doubt I would be able to fit into another church. I have no desire to pastor any other church. If Miller Avenue fired me and another church wanted me, I would have to tell them that they would have to dissolve every piece of their church structure and adopt a simple church government. I would not administrate the committees, boards, and so forth.

The pastoral ministry has one great responsibility and that is to preach the gospel to sinners and saints alike, and to do so we must keep ourselves free of all other entanglements. And there are entanglements, entanglements, and entanglements! In Acts 6 is the story of the apostles' problem administrating distributions to widows. They selected others, the first deacons, to do the job so they could focus on praying and preaching. It is wise to apply Acts 6 as widely as possible.

✜    ✜    ✜    ✜    ✜

☞ If you had your druthers, how would you set up a church in terms of structure?

☞ What changes would you make to the structure you are presently working with?

Twenty-one

# The Worship Service

The note read: "YOUR WORSHIP SERVICE IS BORING!"

Monday evening I called the writer of the note, a visitor, to discuss the disturbing comment. "Can you give me any suggestions?" I asked after a few pleasantries were exchanged. "Yes, too many old hymns, too much Bible stuff, and the sermon was too long." "What would you do instead?" I asked.

He would have gutted the service; he wanted a band, dancing, and multi-media presentations. Nice, I suppose, but beyond our capability.

Our worship service was bound to be boring to this person. I, however, did take the note to the church council for evaluation. In fact, we did spiffy the service up some but probably not enough to satisfy our bored friend.

✣　✣　✣　✣　✣

The worship service is public; that is, visitors are more likely to be present in the worship service than at the prayer meeting or Bible study. It is at the worship service that the gospel will be preached to the unconverted as well as to the converted.

At this point in my ministry I try not to get overly excited about what goes on in the worship service as long as the form and content are biblical. However, the worship service tends to generate more suggestions and criticisms than any other single element in the life of a church. In times past I would be tempted to take any intimation that the service needed to be changed personally. I would defend, argue, and thump my Bible. Now, though, if changes are requested I am more amenable just as long as the teaching and preaching of the gospel remain central. What everyone eventually comes to realize is that there are just so many things that can possibly be done in a service anyway.

Let us consider the worship service. Notice I did not say "Sunday" worship service since some groups worship on days other than Sunday though I think Sunday, the Lord's Day, the day of the resurrection, was normative for the early church (see Acts 20:7, Romans 14:5-6, 1 Corinthians 16:2, Colossians 2:16-17, and Revelation 1:10). A glance at the worship of God as described in the New Testament, and there is very little said about what actually went on in early church services, reveals there were several distinct elements to the worship.

Preaching and teaching were primary. There was prayer, and communion (the Lord's Supper or Eucharist) was observed. Acts 2:42 reads: "They devoted themselves to the apostles' teaching and to the fellowship, to the breaking of bread and to prayer." Psalms where sung, new songs of the Christian community were apparently developed, and there was some free-form music. (See Colossians 3:16 and Ephesians 5:19) In addition, prophecies were given, revelations were announced, and tongues were spoken with interpretation. (See 1 Corinthians 14:26-32) The problem is we know almost nothing about what these forms of worship actually looked like or consisted of. My view is that error may easily result if we read our own contemporary experiences back into the New Testament times. Modern charismatic or Pentecostal understandings of tongues and prophecy may bear little resemblance to the worship of the early church. There are no video or audio recordings of what went on in the church at Corinth or any other New Testament church. Therefore, my conclusion is that I am unsure of what a "scriptural worship service" actually looks like. To be safe I stick with what I am sure of, preaching the gospel, teaching the Scripture, singing the Psalms and other songs that glorify God and lift up Jesus and the cross, praying, celebrating the Lord's Supper, and fellowshipping with believers.

Let me briefly describe a worship service used at Miller Avenue. (Warning: people who are looking to be entertained or are wanting to be in on the "happening" feel-good church do not last long at Miller Avenue.) We begin with a hymn, have a "Call to Worship" followed by a "morning prayer" that is made up by the person who is leading the worship part of the service. After the morning prayer we read the "Collect of the Day" which is a prayer used by millions of Christians of many denominations worldwide, and our version is taken from a Lutheran worship manual. From time to time I will substitute the Lord's Prayer for the collect. Using an overhead projector we sing two or more choruses, old ones and new ones, with a guitar and piano accompanying. All of this is rather sedately done. Our choir makes a presentation after the choruses or perhaps there is a solo or duet. Then comes the memory verse, (I emphasize the memory of Scripture) followed by a point to ponder or reflect upon.

The time for reflection is vital. Moving quickly from one segment of worship to another is not always what people need. Having a time to think, reflect, pray, or simply be silent, can be refreshing and pleasing to many people.

The worship part of the service is over now, total elapsed time about thirty minutes. Announcements come next (I have finally given up on attempts to eliminate announcements), which I view as part of fellowship. During the announcements printed material is often passed out and may include newsletters, testimonies, reprints of helpful articles, and so forth, and any inserts that are in the bulletin are referenced, and recently Spurgeon's Morning and Evening Meditations have been used. (Bulletin covers with pretty pictures seem to be a waste of money and resources; rather, I look for articles and essays that are of some spiritual value to adorn the bulletin cover.) Tithes and offerings are received preceded by a thirty-second presentation of an "offertory theme"—a teaching on biblical giving. Following the offering is a time for "Revelations, Hymns, and Exhortations" (except on Communion Sunday, the first Sunday of the month). Every week I encourage people to bring with them something God has given or shown them during the week in their private devotions or ministry. Of course, this can be risky because someone might say some strange thing or take up an inordinate amount of time, but the risk is worth it. This segment may run five to ten minutes. Bible teaching is next, the Bible Exposition, followed by a second hymn, and then the sermon is preached. The Bible teacher and the sermon preacher may be the same person or two different people. The teaching and preaching may have a similar theme or they may not. Some Sundays a general invitation to prayer for any reason at all is given, prayer for conversion, healing, anything at all. A final hymn serves as a benediction. The entire service will last an hour and fifteen minutes to and hour and a half. The sermon and Bible exposition occupy about half that time.

The service will look different from time to time, and I am generally willing to make changes. Someone asks, "How about this?" I will say, "Okay, let us try that." People will say, "I wish we could change our worship service." My response is, "Okay, what would you like to change? "Things can be changed around a bit, but most changes are basically superficial. Sometimes the announcements are cut out, another hymn is used, or a couple more choruses are sung, the offering is moved to the beginning or the end, more people are involved in the service—small changes really. There is nothing special or sacred about sticking with a particular order of service. The order of worship currently being used is unchanged for at least four years. For most Christians the structure of the worship service is not a great concern; it is the content that matters.

We now have, as of February 2000, a Sunday evening worship service and we call it "The Old-Time Gospel Hour," with all apologies to Jerry Falwell. It begins at 6PM, we sing the great hymns of the Church, preach a strong gospel message, then as many as are up for it, drive over to a local fast food restaurant. This is my favorite service though I put my best effort into the Sunday morning worship service. The evening service, however, allows people who would never be able to attend a morning service, for whatever reason, to hear the gospel preached. I wish I had begun it long ago.

The public prayers in the worship service are traditional and important especially the pastoral prayer, which is prayer for the overall concerns and needs of the congregation. In years gone by this was often a very long prayer, but most are considerably shorter. In any case, public or corporate prayer must be given great attention. Everyone should be able to hear it, and it needs to be sincere and serious. The congregation needs to hear the great concerns of the people of God being lifted up to heaven. Often I have felt unworthy, discouraged, even upset, but when I pray I attempt to put these aside and avoid praying according to my feelings.

The public reading of Scripture is critical; it should be read with all that is due the Word of God. Everyone should be able to hear the words, and they are best spoken somewhat slowly and with emphasis. It is not a dramatic reading that an actor might make, no, but the best the reader has should go into the reading. Perhaps this is the only time during the worship service when people will hear from God. To readers I suggest: prepare, read loudly (best not to depend on a microphone), and read so that people can tell the Bible is being read. Sometimes I have heard people read the Scripture in the same way they might read an advertisement for soap. Much the same can be said for the sermon, which should be delivered with all the intensity and strength we have.

Sunday school—we do not have one but I want to include a suggestion here that has worked for me and may work for others who do not have a Sunday school either.

Most everyone knows what "home-schooling" is. Well, I have simply applied this to the Sunday school. When a family with kids comes along I inform them that we do not have a regular Sunday school but that we will help them home-Sunday school their own kids. At some point we will make this an established ministry of Miller Avenue complete with materials, meetings, and so forth. It is an excellent way to incorporate people with children into the small church when there is no Sunday school in place. And it is quite biblical, too, and may be even better than the typical Sunday school model.

Rather than include a separate chapter on "fellowship" I thought it best to say a word or two on the subject here. One, provide as many opportunities for fellowship as possible. Two, make special efforts to include new people and help them to feel comfortable.

There will be cliques and this is not altogether a bad thing. Cliques can not be helped. Over the course of time a small group of people that regularly meets for whatever purpose will become something of a clique. But it does not have to be a closed group. And this is the key—closedness—whereby new comers are rejected. As long as new people are welcomed, incorporated into the group, then this is a healthy fellowship.

At Miller Avenue we have a light lunch or sometimes simply coffee and tea after the Sunday morning service. For a half-hour or more we sit around and talk together. After the Old-Time Gospel Hour on Sunday evenings we go down to a local fast food place and spend more time together—simply being together—where there is no agenda or topic or plan. Then the Tuesday night Bible study is low-key and there is plenty of time to just talk together. Everyone in the church is not part of the more intimate fellowship times, but they are available for those who desire it.

My job is to provide the opportunity; I can not force people into fellowship.

Outline an order of worship you would use if you could. Which is your favorite part?

☞ Do you think you could bring it to reality?

☞ How might you help a parent organize a home-Sunday school?

Twenty-two

# The Prayer Meeting

"Hello pastor, I am visiting here in Mill Valley and I wondered when your prayer meeting was?"

That question cut me to the quick: we had no prayer meeting.

"My mother is quite ill and I flew in from Miami to be with her. I would like to have some prayer."

I hung up the phone vowing to begin a prayer meeting at Miller Avenue.

✠     ✠     ✠     ✠     ✠

Erroll Hulse has written an excellent tract titled, "The Vital Place of the Prayer Meeting". It may be obtained from the Chapel Library, 2603 W. Wright Street, Pensacola, FL 32505. (This is a ministry of the Mount Zion Bible Church in Pensacola.) I can never do better than what Erroll Hulse has done in that excellent piece of work on the prayer meeting.

Prayer is, of course, vital to the life of the church and to every believer individually. I must admit this is an area in which we are not strong at Miller Avenue Church and I wish this were not the case. However, by the grace of God and the leadership of Anatoli Sokolov, a Baptist pastor and recent immigrant from Moscow,

Russia, we now have a wonderful prayer meeting at Miller Avenue that begins one half hour following the Sunday morning worship service.

Recently I preached a sermon based upon Acts 6:1-6. That passage describes a problem that developed in the primitive church in Jerusalem. The apostles were distracted from vital ministry because of the necessity of caring for the widows of the church. To resolve the situation, the apostles meet with the disciples (the church) and announced, "It would not be right for us to neglect the ministry of the word of God in order to wait on tables." (Verse 2) Thus issued the selection of the first deacons who were assigned the task of serving the widows of the church. The apostles' intent was to focus on "prayer and the ministry of the word." (Verse 4) "Ministry of the word" refers, I believe, to the preaching of the gospel and to the "apostles' teaching". Prayer, preaching, and teaching go together.

In that sermon on Acts 6, I encouraged everyone to make a list of the names of those who were unconverted among their family, friends, and other associates. Alongside the name I suggested noting the date of the initial prayer. The point was to pray regularly for the people whose names were on their list, pray that they would hear the gospel and be converted. I believe that it is important to pray for those we think are unconverted and bring them before the throne of God on a regular basis, pleading that God would draw them to Jesus. The prayer meeting is a likely setting for these prayers.

Our best efforts need to be in the prayer meeting. Not everyone in the church will come to the prayer meeting, but those who delight in prayer and feel the burden of prayer will gather together. The size of the group is irrelevant.

That we are taught to pray is abundantly clear from the Scripture. Through Jesus we have access to the Father who hears our prayer. We are taught to make our needs known to Him, and though He knows our needs before we ask Him, yet we are told to bring our requests to Him.

Prayer has seemed paradoxical to me. The will of God will be done. His purpose will be accomplished because He is the sovereign God, yet in the prayer meeting we bring our requests before the throne of grace and have the confidence that God will hear and that He will act according to His will to bring glory to our Lord Jesus Christ.

It sometimes evolves that the prayer meeting takes on the character of a Bible study or a preaching meeting. However, prayer meetings are best if they are in fact prayer meetings. A prayer meeting need not be lengthy, but it needs to be serious. It has been my experience that the focus should be on prayers for the unconverted, for those who are ill, and for those who need to be encouraged in their faith. We can pray for those who have the rule over us in the secular world. We can pray for Christian leaders around the world and for churches around the world. We can pray for difficult circumstances wherever and whatever they might be. But it is best if it is a time of prayer and not discussion, because we have a tendency to want to discus issues rather than bring them to the Lord in heartfelt prayer.

There are many forms the prayer meeting might take. Let me suggest three of the most common. One, after a short exhortation to prayer or the reading of a verse on prayer, various people can bring any request before God aloud while the others listen to and "agree" with the prayer. Two, either sitting or kneeling, each person can pray aloud or silently, and this perhaps after a short word or two on the subject of prayer. Some of the best prayer meetings I have ever been in have been small and we have been on our knees. It was in such a prayer meeting that God called me into the ministry. Three, a prayer request is made then someone in the group recalls a promise in Scripture that speaks to the request. For example, a request is made for new Sunday school teachers and then another person (or the same person) reminds the group of the saying of Jesus: "The harvest is plentiful but the workers are few. Ask the Lord of the harvest, therefore, to send out workers into his harvest field" (Matthew 9:37-38). Then the specific prayers are made. This pattern can continue until the meeting time expires. (I think it is best if there is a definite ending point and that the leader adheres to it.) There are, of course, many more forms for the prayer meeting.

Many wonderful things happen in prayer meetings. During the Third Great Awakening in America, 1858-1860, the prayer meeting was central, more so than even preaching. Somehow we are more sensitive to God's Holy Spirit at prayer; our hearts may become tender and open to the words of Jesus. I believe the Holy Spirit impresses upon us the truth of His word in that quiet, rare, and wonderful time when we turn our heart, soul, and mind to the Lord, coming into His very presence.

☞ Can you remember a prayer meeting where you had the sense that you were in the presence of God?

☞ Few have I suppose. What prayer meeting format seems best to you?

Twenty-three

# The Bible Study

"You take the Bible way too literally for me. I am shopping around and I know Miller Avenue isn't my kind of church. I am not interested in what happened to a bunch of Jews a long time ago."

Absolutely correct, Miller Avenue would not work for this person. Should I change to accommodate him? Should I suddenly become "liberal" so that I might get this person into a pew?

✢　✢　✢　✢　✢

The early Christians were devoted to the "apostles' teaching". (See Acts 2:42) At that point in the history of the Church it would have meant a devotion to the words and deeds of Jesus as well as to the entire Hebrew Scripture, the Old Testament. In our time we look to our Bible, the Old and New testaments, for the apostles' teaching.

What an incredible document the Bible is, a never-ending supply of wisdom and grace. The Bible is God's very word that the Holy Spirit helps us to understand. The Bible is a book about Jesus, His past, His present, and His future. However, it is "spiritually hidden" from the unconverted and often mysterious to the converted so the ministry of exposing the Bible is indeed a critical one.

Since 1968 I have had the blessed privilege of teaching a Tuesday night Bible study. The name of my little television program is "The Bible Study". In both cases I teach verse by verse, starting from where I left off and ending wherever we happen to be when time runs out.

Preparation for the Bible study is nearly as extensive as for the sermon. The actual Bible study lasts for one and a half hours while the television program is only one half hour. My study for the television program is simply a perusal of the material from the Bible study, and that is usually not much more than a few notes in the margins of my study Bible.

Most often the Bible study takes place in my living room. At times it has been conducted in the church building. It is informal and as relaxed as I can make it. Sometimes I have hot water ready for coffee, tea, or otherwise, with some cookies or fruit. Not many come, five to eight people is typical. The material is fairly involved in that I do not gear it for beginners, but I will answer any and all questions. I use no aids or other books though I am not against this and have done so at various times. The Bible study guides, however, seem to get in the way and are usually superficial. People end up studying the guides and/or outlines rather than the Bible itself.

My job is to expose the Scripture. Sometimes I don't understand some passage myself; I am often baffled. I will ask tough questions, even play the role of "devil's advocate" to help people focus on the text and context. As best I can I will avoid interpreting the Scripture to meet the confines of some theological model. The Scripture must say what it says and not what I want it to say. There is no effort on my part to entertain, excite, or inspire; this must come naturally, or supernaturally, from the Word of God itself. As we hear Jesus speaking to us from His Word, we are changed. Hearing Philpott helps no one.

It is my general practice to begin on time, often without an opening prayer, and close with a prayer. Starting from the opening verse I will proceed until someone asks a question or makes a comment. It is not intended to be a lecture and if need be I will ask questions myself to provoke discussion. There is no offering, no personal ministry such as praying for people for healing, and so on. Bible study is just that; Bible studies have been known to "deteriorate" into preaching meetings or discussion groups.

Let me suggest several forms the Bible study might take. One, much as I have described above, my own method. Two, various people are assigned passages that they are then to expose with a leader keeping things on track. Three, the study of major themes of a biblical book rather than a verse by verse approach. Four, personal profiles of major biblical characters are presented. Five, people are invited to present their favorite biblical passages with discussion of the same conducted by the leader. There are, of course, many other Bible study methods. I do not want to make it seem that I am against the very fine Bible study outlines and guides current today. These can be used to great advantage.

The history of the world for a thousand years before the Reformation has been called the "Dark Ages." The availability of the Scripture to the common person brought light into the darkness. The Bible is not to be worshipped or used as a weapon, yet the Bible is a great treasure to be studied diligently and loved greatly.

✢    ✢    ✢    ✢    ✢

☞ If you could keep it secret, would you describe you real attitude toward the Bible?

☞ How do you feel about it? Do you feel confident as a teacher of the Bible?

☞ What problems do you have with the Bible?

Twenty-four

# Avoid Political and Social Controversies

"Pastor, we as a church have got to get the vote out this year and we need to promote the Christian candidates. And that proposition supporting capital punishment is the most important one of all."

"Pastor, we as a church have got to get the vote out this year and we need to promote the Christian candidates. And that proposition against capital punishment is the most important one of all."

✢　✢　✢　✢　✢

There are many political and social controversies, causes, and issues that churches become embroiled in. Some are extremely worth while, some are even important.

There is no end of Christian based programs and movements that have a political or social dimension and are generally approved of in the Christian community. These, however, tend to divert and dilute the message and ministry of the gospel preacher.

Christians are often pictured as being politically conservative; this identification is not always a helpful one. People will reject the Christian message for no other reason than they think political baggage goes along with it. And, the fact is that perception is too often correct.

Of course, Jesus is not identified with any political party. And though many Christians might fall into politically conservative camps, Christianity itself is not political. Espousing certain political views, endorsing political candidates (while it may seem to be expedient and often-times even demanded in certain environments) will ultimately prejudice the gospel to the very people who need to hear it's message.

Political opinions and positions are sometimes mixed right in with gospel presentations. The message seems to be, "*Choose Jesus and support so and so and such and such.*" What a mistake! An unnecessary obstacle is placed in the way of the unconverted as though the gospel were not offense enough.

People at Miller Avenue do not know how I vote or what political party I identify with (I hope). Neither political material nor speakers come before the congregation. Christians, certainly, are to be good citizens and may take active roles in politics, but the gospel preacher is neither a politician nor a promoter of political causes. I like to think our job is far too important than for us to be bogged down in secular trivia.

Christianity, as I have said before, is worldwide, cross-cultural, and not identified with any political party or cause. Christianity is not Western, it is not Eastern; it is global. Jesus died that all people may come to Him as Savior. Potentially any one in the world may come to Jesus, regardless of their political affiliation or their social commitments.

There are several social concerns I avoid though many Christians are heavily immersed in them. Although I have particular views on abortion, I will not get drawn into that arena. My views tend to be conservative in that regard, yet the issue has been politicized to the point that I think spending time, money, and energy in that direction is largely counter productive. I also will avoid the issues of capital punishment and prayer in the schools. (I am probably limiting the audience for this book by stating my feelings like this.) These are not areas where I want to stand up on a bandwagon and start beating the drum. My finding is that once exposed to the Scripture, by the leading of the Holy Spirit, Christians tend to come to certain conclusions on social, political, and ethical issues without my having to influence them myself. Certain stances become obvious.

Christians have a number of different views on the ethical and social issues; I have mine, but they are not ones I am going to be speaking on from the pulpit. A safe illustration is that during the "Cold War" I did not demonize the Soviet Union nor preach fear of communism though I reject the system. I think it is very important that we learn to *agree to disagree* about things that are not central to the gospel message. Now I know that there will be those that will argue against me, but this is my opinion. I believe we need to speak out against sin and take various stands, but the promotion of the gospel must remain uncontaminated by other messages.

Another area I don't get involved in is the *Evolution verses Creationist* controversy. I believe the Biblical account in Genesis—God as maker of heaven and earth—and I pretty much leave it at that. I have not always done so, but I have found it to be an area that is overwhelming, and people can become greatly obsessed with this issue. In my experience, people who were atheistic evolutionists, upon hearing the message of the gospel, have been converted and became followers of Jesus. I find that I do not need to deal with the various views they have. People's social and political views have a way of changing as time goes on especially as a person is exposed to the Scripture. What I cannot do through providing videos and books and cassette tapes and argument, God's Spirit can do. If a person differs with me on some point, this does not greatly excite or concern me. I do not want to be the agent for change; rather I would have that be God's province.

A pastor who focuses on conversion oriented gospel preaching, I observe, generally will not engage themselves, except minimally, in extraneous controversies even within their own denomination. We only have so much time, so much energy, and it is too easy to be distracted by the "significant" trivialities we are constantly faced with. And there is one issue right after another. Let others engage in those things; but let us go forward proclaiming the gospel, lifting up the name of Jesus, and somehow these other things get taken care of along the way as well.

☞ Did I tread on any of your favorite issues?

☞ If I did, can you separate that from the basic thrust of the chapter?

☞ What happens when politics, social issues, and the gospel are all mixed up together?

Twenty-five

# Avoid "Movements" Within Christianity

"Today we are going to hear from Brother Blank who will report on the new thing God is doing in His Church."

"Hundreds of Christian leaders gathered in Los Angeles over the weekend to learn how to prepare for the upcoming computer meltdown."

"Some churches are becoming '12 Step' centered. It shows we can learn from the culture we live in."

✠　　✠　　✠　　✠　　✠

In the 37 years I have been a Christian, I have seen many "movements" come and go. For instance, there have been prophecy movements; Christians excited about world events that surely signal the soon return of Jesus. Books about the "YK2" problem were big in 1999. I have seen movements for the "Battle for the Bible," people getting excited about defending the Bible. I have seen movements regarding shepherding, preaching the necessity of being submitted to a "shepherd," which would result in a balanced life. I have seen the "Deliverance Movement"—everyone getting all the demons cast out. (I was involved in this particular movement myself.)

120

Then I have seen the movements whereby addictions are cured or healed. (Almost everyone is an addict, so we are told, and we can be free of them by doing such and such.) And so we have Christian movements that focus on addictions.

There has been a large and popular movement whereby oaths and promises are made thus insuring true Christian manhood. And spiritually discerning Christians are "mapping" the demons that control cities and that frustrate the success of the gospel message. There have been, there are, and there will be "movements" within the Christian community.

The Christian community, by and large, seems to constantly need to be excited by some new thing. A big revival is talked about here, and people are learning how to take over their local governments over there; people are rushing off to someplace in Canada, or they are going off to someplace in Florida. They are booking airplane flights and making hotel reservations. They are spending lots of money running off and having a good time then coming back and trying to get their churches to appreciate the new movement and get on board.

New movements have to be sold to the church, and pastors end up being promoters rather than preachers. Literature is mailed out, meetings are called, and special speakers are brought in—all to get people on track with the new and exciting movement. Talk about a waste of resources!

Nearly all of the movements I have ever seen turn out to be somehow funny and strange, but more than that they are diversions from the primary goal of the gospel ministry. Movements waste our money, steal our time, and embarrass us. My suggestion is to avoid movements.

Could it be that those who are merely Christianized (those who experience false conversion) are the ones who are attracted to the movements within Christianity? It has been my observation that those who have experienced true conversion are satisfied with Jesus. Growing up into the stature of the fullness of Jesus and bringing Him glory and honor, these seem to be enough.

The work of the gospel preacher is always full and never ending. Therefore there is usually little time for the movements, exciting events, great meetings, and outstanding seminars with so many great speakers coming together. Well, these may keep people excited, moving and supposedly busy, but I wonder about the movements.

☞ What "movements" have you gotten involved with?

☞ Where are those movements now?

Brain storm to see if you can guess what the next one will be. I think it will involve celebrations and rituals. Yes, Christians seem to be captivated by big, noisy, "spiritual" celebrations.

Twenty-six

# Avoid Fund-raisers

"This will help so many in our church. I know a couple people who could earn some extra money and it will be good for fellowship. And, pastor, you could save some money, too."

It sounded too good to be true. Guess what! It was.

✠   ✠   ✠   ✠   ✠

Rarely a week goes by that I am not contacted by phone about a fund-raiser. A major industry has developed around fund-raising, and of course, fund-raising companies target churches.

Fund-raising businesses purchase lists of nonprofit organizations, and the opening tactic is to send out a couple of slick brochures followed some days later by a phone call. And they will have a fund-raiser guaranteed to bring in lots of money. For example, they will produce a directory for the church complete with photos. They will handle everything. Everyone will get a nice directory and for every order $5.00 comes to the church. It works, too. This is usually no scam; it's just that the program has to be run through the governing process, and promoted, and then promoted some more. Usually there is some paper work, phone calling, and ruffled feathers to be soothed, too.

Or there is a deal for long-distance phone rates and the church will get a certain percentage. Or perhaps it is group life or medical insurance, and the church members will get a break on the premiums plus a certain percentage of the premiums paid come directly to the church. The word is, "Simply wonderful, a win-win situation". And there are dozens of schemes, often operated by Christian organizations, even missionary enterprises. I am amazed at the creativity of these people; they have almost every angle down.

The appeals are irresistible; some people get quite excited about raising money for the choir or a youth program, and "We really do need to repave the parking lot". In general, the support of special projects, especially onetime events, may be okay. But the principle I try to stick to is—no fund-raising for the general budget. The tithes and offerings that come in at the regularly appointed meetings and services alone must support the budget.

There are always reasons for fund-raisers, sometimes compelling reasons. After the package is agreed to then the work of promoting the fund-raiser must begin; the concept has to be sold to the people. There will be meetings, meetings with committees and boards and councils; of course, everyone must be "on board". It will be necessary to allot a significant amount of Sunday morning announcement time, at least, for promotional purposes. It will be in the bulletin for weeks, special flyers will be printed, posters painted and banners made—to get everyone excited about the fund-raiser.

Once one fund-raiser is run there will likely be more of them. The budget may come to depend on fund-raisers. "We are going to make up our red ink through a fund-raiser." Then there will be a lot of fund-raisers. It is a tremendously draining exercise.

Now I will admit that Miller Avenue does do a yard sale once a year for our Annual Gospel Concert. (I am not as clean here as it might seem.) The yard sale is a compromise on my part and I have not made up my mind whether I am doing the right thing or not. For the last nine years we have had an annual yard sale to fund the concert. I have to admit it is fun to do. All of the money goes directly to our gospel concert. But I have at least limited fund-raising to the concert. I say "No" to everything else though some are quite tempting.

Despite my inconsistency, my suggestion is to avoid fund-raisers, particularly anything that has to do with saving money on telephone rates, insurance, utilities, soap, cosmetics, plastic containers, and groceries—anything where people sign up and change who it is they have been doing business with.

Of course, many promoters of fund-raisers are certain it is all for Jesus. One hears, "Don't you want your money go to Christians rather than those pagan, secular utility companies?" Well, I got sold once; I tried a telephone deal. A slick start-up telecommunications company in the south someplace sold me, and all *for the glory of God.*

I got a whole bunch of people to switch their long-distance telephone carriers to this wonderful Christian group. We did a promotion, a company representative even flew out; we had a couple of meetings and people got excited about it and changed their long-distance telephone carrier. The company made one point very clear—there would be no charge to make the switch. We had it in writing. Praise God! And then the long distance bill was going to be lowered by 20% and 10%

of that total would come right into the church. Imagine 10% right into the church!

It's simple really. Let's say the long-distance phone bill had been $50.00 a month. The new company would save the subscriber $10 and $5.00 would come right into the church. Praise God! Come right here into the church! Well, we did it, and I persuaded nearly all of the elderly people in the church to get on board. We were going to use the money for the choir. This was actually the plan to fund the gospel concert before we came up with the yard sale idea.

The first thing that happened, people come to me and complained they had been charged, I think $10.00, to switch over; and of course, that was not supposed to happen. When I contacted the company they apologized for the charges and said they couldn't help it, it was the FCC, or something or other, the NCA, or the TWP, or some kind of government agency that charged this and, well, what can you do. We had that little hurdle.

The next thing people reported that their long-distance phone bills had jumped considerably. I contacted the company again and said, "We were supposed to have a 20% saving." I was told, "You know that comes in the second year. We haven't quite got there." I checked my notes at that point and this was indeed news.

When after several months had elapsed and no money had come into the church I called again. I said, "It has been four months now and we have not received a check. We figure it ought to be forty or fifty bucks by now, for the choir." And the voice at the other end said, "We are going to look into this." They looked into it for more than six months. The last time I called I got a recording saying the phone had been disconnected.

We never did receive a single penny. Everybody had to switch back over to their old long distance carrier and it cost them another $10.00 apiece. It was a complete boondoggle. In fact, a couple of years went by before we finally got that company to keep reenlisting us as their customers. We told them over and over "We do not want you to be our long distance carrier." No matter, they kept doing it, the $10 switching charges continued and there are some people who are still mad at me. It ultimately cost the Philpott's around a hundred dollars and a lot of prestige, and it was a long time before the people on the church council would listen to anything I brought up about money.

Flee fund-raisers!

☞ Anybody have a story you could send me about a fund-raiser?

Maybe someone had a good experience—tell me about it.

☞ How would you handle it if a person in the congregation announced that he or she had the perfect idea for a fund-raiser?

Twenty-seven

# Limit Promotions

"I just got a letter from our missionaries in South America and they need a new computer and a new truck. I figure it will run about $12,000. Pastor, what are you going to do about it?"

"I think I will simply scrape a little bit more gold off the chandelier."

✤　✤　✤　✤　✤

Pastors are asked, sometimes expected, to promote many important and worthy causes: in some instances it seems more like a demand than a request. Before I learned how to say "No," I spent an inordinate amount of time begging for money. Squeezing money out of people seemed like a major feature of my job.

Of course I present the need for giving tithes and offerings. In the Sunday morning bulletin I routinely have an offertory theme. Sometimes the theme coordinates with the sermon, sometimes it does not. The offertory theme provides an opportunity for a brief teaching on giving. In addition, a record of the week by week giving is presented in the Sunday bulletin. The monthly newsletter contains a complete accounting of the giving and spending for the past month.

Miller Avenue is part of a particular denomination, and the denomination has four offerings a year. We participate in the "The One Great Hour of Sharing" offering, an America for Christ offering (home missions), the World Mission offering (foreign missions), and an offering for retired ministers and missionaries. This is characteristic of American Baptist Churches. Prior to the date of the offering, I receive a box of promotional materials, videos, cassette tapes, posters, and bulletin inserts. A financial goal is set, an educational and motivational process is set in motion, and the goal is usually met.

Beside the four basic denominational offerings there are others we promote as well. Several of the missionary organizations we give to usually send a representative around once a year to promote their work and take up a love offering. In addition, there are other important groups who make requests to come before the congregation and present their ministries. And then there are the local charities and outreaches; they too, look to churches for support. The over-riding need is money, sometimes money and volunteers.

It is difficult for me to make evaluations about the worthiness of a ministry or outreach. What makes it even more stressful is that friends will be entreating me to support their ministry. However, limitations must be made, pastors must learn to say, "I wish I could". If not, the pastor will continually be asking the congregation for money.

A common perception, for Christians and non-Christians alike, is that the church is simply after money. This perception is not far from the truth. We are too often either taking an offering or preparing to take one.

It is essential to limit promotions. There will be some promotion certainly, and my suggestion is to select one or two or three a year and do a sensible promotion. And be very straightforward about it: "We are going to raise money for _____ and here is the reason why." Giving, I have found, will actually increase when the constant selling, promoting, and persuading is limited. Above all, reject any tactic that tends to make people feel guilty for not giving.

Though this does not logically belong at the end of this chapter, I want to include a tangential issue. I think it is extremely important that no one know what anyone else in the church is giving. Certainly the church treasurer is going to know, and consequently that church treasurer needs to be a confidential person who will not divulge information. And the treasurer must not act towards someone in a deferential manner on the basis of giving.

Pastors do not want to know who gives what! I do not know who gives what and I do not care who gives what. It matters not if a person gives a dollar or a thousand dollars a month; I will not pay attention to the one person over the other. It is a mistake to do so. Too easily we can get into a situation where we are afraid of losing somebody we know is a substantial financial contributor. Such a person can then wield an unhealthy power over us. We want to reject that kind of fear and entanglement.

✢   ✢   ✢   ✢   ✢

☞ Do you have strong feelings about money and the church?

☞ Perhaps the worst experience is having to promote an offering for a cause you do not care for. Have you a plan for limiting promotions?

Twenty-eight

# What Title to Use

"How shall we refer to you on the wedding announcement?"

"I like 'Most Holy Reverend Doctor'. It has a ring to it don't you think?"

✧　✧　✧　✧　✧

Just what or who are we? The usual titles are "reverend," "minister," or "pastor," and some like to use "Doctor" if they have an earned doctorate. Though I have an earned doctorate, a DMin., (not an academic, but practical degree) I do not use it. It sounds pretentious. I reserve "Doctor" for medical doctors, dentists, and other medical specialists. But I will use the term, also, for university, college, or seminary professors if they have an earned Ph.D. or Th.D., but that is about it. I restrict my use of the title because I noticed that I was too pleased with being called "Dr. Philpott".

One day I introduced myself as Doctor Philpott to a small group that included a rather well known medical doctor. The M.D. gave his name, Doctor so-and-so. It embarrassed me. He intended, I felt, to embarrass me. He knew my doctorate had something to do with theology, and he could, I think, sense the kind of self-important way in which I announced myself. That was the last time I pulled that. I do not use the title in the Yellow Pages of the telephone book, and I do not use the term on my stationary or my business card. I have no quarrel with others who do use it, however.

"Pastor" is the designation I use. I do not like the title "reverend" maybe because I do not feel very reverent most of the time. And I do not know what "reverend" means exactly except that it is a ministerial designation. The term "minister" is appropriate. When I sign a wedding document (at least the ceremonial certificate) I declare that I am a "Minister of the Gospel."

Essentially my function is to pastor a church, so that is the title I use. When I meet people for the first time they often don't know how to address me. I will generally extend my hand and say, "My name is Kent Philpott" thereby letting them know how I prefer to be called. If people ask "How am I to introduce you?" or "How am I to list you on the program?" I will say, "After my name should read, 'pastor.'" And if they want more than that I say, "Pastor of Miller Avenue Baptist Church." But generally, upon introduction, I give my full name without title.

The question comes up, "How are kids to refer to you?" I may not have the right spin on this, but I just introduce myself to them as "Kent". If a parent wants to say, "This is Pastor Philpott", or "Pastor Kent", or "Reverend Philpott" I let it go at that. However parents wants to instruct their child to refer to me I will accept. I will not correct a child but will let them call me anything they want to.

Robes, clerical robes—though not the subject of this chapter, I do not want to come up with a separate chapter about robes—deserve some comment. I have worn robes yet never felt comfortable with them. One Sunday morning I tripped on the stole on my way up to the pulpit and thereby generated a chorus of giggles. I would not mention this topic except that I have met too many ministers who take what I consider to be too great a delight in dressing up in robes and other religious garments. Robes were developed in an era when the office of minister was undergoing a transition from servant to shaman, or servant to magician. Special garments symbolized extra ordinary powers. That is one theory anyway, and another is that robes help set the ministry apart or call attention to the specialness of Christian ministry. I have little objection to this latter view, but clothes should not be what makes the ministry special.

If a particular denomination or church traditionally uses robes, fine, ignore what I have said here all the while keeping in mind our tendency to think of ourselves more highly than we ought.

☞ What title do you prefer?

☞ What does the old term, "puffed up" mean to you?

Twenty-nine

# On Being a Counselor

"Kent, remember what I told you about my mother. You've got to promise me that you will never tell another living soul. I'll just die if you do."

"I assure you, I will never mention it to anyone, not even my wife."

(One month later.)

"Kent, now my husband knows. You must have told him because no one else knew. How could you? I'll never trust you again."

✛ ✛ ✛ ✛ ✛

My college major was psychology. I left a graduate program in counseling to attend Golden Gate Baptist Theological Seminary. It seemed natural enough to combine pastoral ministry and counseling; I perceived of myself as a pastor/counselor.

Following my involvement in the "Jesus Movement" I developed a counseling ministry, in the 70's particularly, called the Marin Christian Counseling Center. Christian counseling was a subject of great interest during that particular time and, of course, it continues to be. As a pastor with counseling skills I thought I would be able to help people overcome emotional and spiritual based problems. For ten years I spent four days a week with as many as six, seven, sometimes eight appointments a day. All kinds of people made appointments—people in the church, people outside the church, Christians, and non-Christians. I never charged a penny.

People would reveal their innermost secrets, deep dark stuff, sometimes details of their lives they really hadn't intended to divulge; it would just come out. Too often I would know way too much.

During the counseling process itself revelations of past events did not seem to pose any threat. However, I now had information that might prove damaging should it get out. Even the closest relationships are subject to strain, and sensitive, personal information disclosed in a counseling situation may be problematic once the strength of the counseling bond diminishes. This is especially applicable for pastors who do in-depth (more than simple pastoral ministry) counseling with members of the congregation.

I have discovered that when people go through a life crisis and disclose intimate details of their lives, though it seems okay at the time, when the crisis is past, they may be embarrassed and uncomfortable in the pastor's presence. It may even be necessary for the person to find another church. This has happened to me more than once. Therefore, I have determined not to be a counselor or confessor if I can avoid it.

People will confess their sins and if such repentance arises naturally out of the Holy Spirit's conviction, well and good. But to set oneself up as a qualified counselor, one ready to hear and handle the deep, dark, complicated things—I think this is a mistake for the pastor.

We are called into the pastoral ministry not into the work of the psychotherapist, analyst, or counselor. When, however, someone lays a problem before me and asks for advice or counsel I respond, "I am not a counselor, I am not a therapist, and I receive no compensation for counseling." (I ought also to disclose that I have neither a license nor malpractice insurance.)

It is not unusual for a person who is not a member of my congregation to offer to pay me for my time. My answer is: "There is no charge. If you want to make a donation to the church, you can." And I will only say that if absolutely pressed. I prefer that no money change hand at all.

Pastoral ministry is what I will do, however. I can tell a person what the Scripture says about a particular issue, I can pray with and for somebody, I can relate some of the things I have learned in my life and ministry, but beyond that I hope not to go. I will listen carefully, I will actively share what I feel is helpful, and I may be able to recommend someone who would be better qualified and trained than myself.

And so it is that I don't want to know too much about an individual. I want to be the pastor/teacher. I do not want to be the counselor. Pastoral psychology and counseling are taught in our seminaries and Bible colleges and I am not saying that is an error or wrong. I'm saying simply that as a pastor I would rather not engage in it.

As I have already stated, I get to know more than I ever wanted to know acting as a counselor, but secondly, it is an extraordinarily time-consuming process. Not only does counseling require large blocks of time, it is emotionally draining as well. To hear of the pain, suffering, and grief of others is a difficult thing. What is it that is said, "Psychiatrists have the highest suicide rate of any profession." Whether this is true or not I don't know, but I know there is an incredibly high attrition rate for people who engage in psychotherapeutic work.

The job of the pastoral minister is to preach the gospel and help those who are converted to grow up into the stature of the fullness of Jesus. And people are to work out their own salvation with fear and trembling. I don't want to have a person develop a relationship with me that they really need to have with Jesus. I would rather have them view Jesus as their counselor. Jesus is the Counselor, the Advocate, the Paraclete, the One who comes alongside to help. I would rather see an individual develop a strong devotional life and learn to trust the Lord to be their counselor. I am then free to be the pastor/teacher.

☞ Do you want to function as a counselor?

☞ Do you perceive a difference between pastoral counsel and the counsel of a licensed therapist?

☞ Have you experienced the betrayal of confidence?

Thirty

# On Helping Others

"Hello pastor, my children and I are at the Fireside Motel and we are stuck. We're trying to get to my parent's home in Portland and the car won't work. We haven't eaten in two days and we're out of money. Can you help?"

"Kent, I need about $400 to pay the rent. I'll be glad to do some work around the church if I can have the money."

"Pastor, my neighbors are out of work and their kids need food money. Do we have a benevolence fund?"

Every pastor is familiar with requests like those above. For the small church pastor, especially, these are some of the most agonizing of all situations.

✣    ✣    ✣    ✣    ✣

The subject of this chapter is how giving might be a blessing and a ministry, not a curse. Here are a few ideas on helping others.

Miller Avenue Baptist Church is located on Miller Avenue in Mill Valley, one of the main streets of our town (about 13,000 people). It is a busy street and I keep the front door open. I open it up in the morning and I close it in the evening. Anyone may come in and pray and read the Bible. There is a small table in the foyer with a rack that is generally filled with free literature along with some Bibles.

Our building is small. My office can easily be seen from the foyer; it has the word "Pastor" over the door. The result is people will occasionally knock on my office door hoping to receive some kind of assistance.

In times past we had a pastor's or benevolence fund. We put $50.00 a month into it. By the end of the first week, generally, the fund was exhausted. If the church committed $500.00 a month to a benevolence fund, the money would be gone in a very short time.

Let me illustrate why I feel a benevolence fund is problematic. The given: $50 (or whatever) to give out each month. A person asks for some help because they are in desperate trouble. The $50 is now gone. The treasurer will not replenish the fund until the first part of the coming month. Then another person comes in, someone in the church for instance, and now the pastor has to report that the money is gone. What suspicions or feelings of rejection might be generated in the mind of that member of the church family?

Our church council gives me permission to give up to $100.00 away without their approval if there is a genuine need. (I recently exceeded that amount and got into some trouble.) But I do not like to have such authority. It is so difficult to determine the authenticity of a situation since there usually is no time or reliable means to make inquiries. And certainly, there is no way to run all of the requests for money though the church council. If the council investigated all the requests for benevolence, there would be little if any time left for other matters.

My solution is to only give my money away. I generally have a five or ten-dollar bill, or maybe even a twenty-dollar bill, in my desk that I can give. It is very hard for me to give tithes and offerings to people who could just as easily be telling me a story. But I will give a little of my money away.

And I give it away; I do not make a loan. Giving a loan, particularly to somebody in the church, is a first class mistake! People, now in debt, have a cloud and a burden hanging over them. Additionally, people who get themselves into financial trouble often have that need exist for quite some time—it is rarely a onetime fix.

It has been my unhappy experience that a debtor will leave the church with nothing more than a note saying they will pay the money back as quickly as possible. I've had that happen enough that I learned not to loan money. When money is handed out to meet a need, it should be a gift, whether the money is given to a person in the church or to a stranger who knocks on the door.

I don't mind giving away a five or ten-dollar bill. And I've heard everything: transmission broken down, engine blown up, electricity turned off, no food in the house, operation desperately needed, severe toothache, on and on. My money is not going to make much of a difference in such a case. I do have a list of organizations, public and private, that may be able to provide additional assistance. But I do not make a judgement on the worthiness of the need. Even when I think I am being taken, I will often hand over a five-dollar bill.

Sometimes I must simply say to a person in need, "I wish I could help". And I mean those words; I wish I could fix the world and make all the pain and suffering go away. I am doing little more than taking note of the person's need and expressing the desire that if I could I would do something to alleviate the problem.

I set aside roughly $50.00 a month of my own money that I use for either offerings (giving to people who ask for it) or I will buy things so I don't have to go to the treasurer all the time. Very few people know I do this, but it has served me well for 15 years.

My favorite way of helping others is to do practical things. Later I suggest that pastors have a pickup truck; indeed, one of my specialties is moving and hauling things with my truck. Sometimes a seemingly small thing can be a great blessing. I recall a person who needed to take dozens of plastic bags full of garbage and other debris to the dump. The job, completed in an hour, turned out to be a great time of fellowship.

Experienced pastors understand the "ministry of presence". Being there, only being present, is sometimes the entire ministry that is needed, or wanted. In my earlier years I was a persistent advice giver. Now my aim is to avoid giving advice even when it is asked for. All my supposed wisdom and profound insight may serve only to get in the way and obscure issues. My concern is to listen and reflect back what I hear. Pastors are not therapists or social workers though we dabble in both; it is better to be a loving and caring friend who can lift needs up to the throne of God in heartfelt prayer.

We will not be able to fill every need. The reality is we may not be able to help even in desperate situations. After we have done all we can we may yet feel like we've failed. Hardly a week goes by but I am confronted with a sense of inadequacy in the face of human need. I can't sell the building nor move everyone into the parsonage. I am learning to face my limitations and, at the same time, not succumb to guilt or despair. We will always have the poor and hurting with us, and we will do our best for them, as we are able.

✢     ✢     ✢     ✢     ✢

It is probably clear that I am far from an expert when it comes to human need.

☞ Do you have ideas on how to strengthen this chapter, perhaps some ideas on dealing with a sense of failure and inadequacy when we have no resources?

Thirty-one

# Recognition and Rewards

"You did not mention me in your newsletter. I did as much as anyone else."

No question, I had inadvertently left his name out. I apologized and righted the slight during the announcements the very next Sunday morning. But he was not there to hear it. In fact, I have not seen him since.

There is something in my flesh that loves to be noticed and admired. I want to be appreciated, talked about, lifted up, and applauded. How I enjoy recognition. The flesh cries out for it, yet, God's glory will not be shared. So many of us have fallen so very far when we were so very well known.

The gospel preacher, as anyone else, must face the desire (need even) to be noticed and recognized. Some will say these are normal needs and perfectly acceptable. In any case, a great deal of energy goes into recognizing people's efforts and contributions.

What recognition does the servant deserve? We are called to be servants of Jesus; Paul referred to himself as "a slave of Jesus." It is biblically legitimate to refer to all Christians as "slaves of Christ." (see Ephesians 6:6) What kind of recognition is due the slave?

There were some religious people of Jesus' day who liked to be noticed. They wore special garments that marked them as religious people. They made long prayers in public, and Jesus said, "They have received their reward in full" (Matthew 6:5). Not much of a reward, is it? —to be honored by people for appearance and performance. Preachers of the gospel must not relish dressing in religious garments and esteeming the "salutations in the market place".

Praise and adulation sought from people seem so unbecoming the gospel minister. I do not see in Scripture that we are called to seek attention and recognition. Paul said that apostles had "become the scum of the earth, the refuse of the world" (1 Corinthians 4:13). Paul may well have had a need for recognition but he saw it for what it was—something inconsistent with servant-hood. Pastors, as well as apostles, may have the same view of themselves. The call to be a slave of Jesus is the highest of callings and is its own reward.

People can be manipulated because of their desire for attention and recognition. At Miller Avenue I attempt to avoid using recognition processes in such ways. However, people will be recognized in the normal course of things without intentional promotion. Service done in the name of Jesus and for His glory may, in fact, be recognized. We know this by looking at the history of the Church. Many faithful men and women are yet recognized for their service to Christ, long after their death. Certainly this is the exception rather than the rule. Most Christians live out their entire lives in obscurity. Many Christians have labored long years in mission fields with little outward results.

Their names are lost to us today and more than likely lost to the generation that immediately followed them. In most instances heroes of the faith (from a heavenly point of view) were unknown during their own time and perhaps were even despised or ignored, but they continued to labor. I doubt these served Jesus in order to obtain recognition or attention. The Christian worker takes on the "easy" yoke of Jesus for the sake of Jesus Himself and for His glory. Striving for recognition and earthly reward is vain and in vain.

People's need for recognition may become a problem in the church. When a system of rewarding service is in place, people may become confused about why they are engaging in ministry. This may seem to be a harsh analysis. I must admit that it has not always been true, in my own personal experience, that recognition processes become problematic.

The "reward and punishment" process is a powerful one. When people are rewarded and recognized for the time and/or money they give they may come to depend on that. If the reward system fails somehow, this person may feel punished. To be quite clear, I have found some workers in the church will "pick up their marbles and go home" if they do not receive what they consider to be sufficient reward. When someone begins to serve in the church I wonder if they will continue if they are unrecognized for it.

So many of the ministries of the church are not public. Few of the gifts of the Holy Spirit, as they are expressed, are public in their application. The ministry of administration, helps, mercy, these and others are largely behind- the-scene ministries where there may be no public recognition at all. The person whose service is done to honor God is the kind of person a pastor appreciates working with. To make the point one more time, people who have a constant need for attention and recognition are people to beware of, because they will never receive enough. It must be enough that we are counted worthy to share in the ministry of Jesus simply for the privilege of being able to honor our Lord with our lives.

For a few years I was not in ministry, and I found that to serve the Lord was the one thing that I loved to do above all things. To be able to preach the gospel, to teach the Scripture, to serve other Christians—these are the precious things. And whether we are recognized is not essential. If attention and recognition come, so be it, if it does not come, then with that we need to be content.

☞ Do you know what it is to be "slighted?"

☞ How well do you like attention and recognition?

☞ Do you feel I went too far in depreciating recognition?

147

Thirty-two

# Coping with Failure

"I'm not a cry-baby or a whiner, but this is awful. I don't think I'm going to be able to make it. Even my kids want me to quit. Tell me, Kent, you have been through desperate times, how do you keep going?"

✢　✢　✢　✢　✢

I wish I had the statistics on the attrition rate in the pastoral ministry. I'll bet it is high, maybe staggeringly so. It's no job for those who are afraid of failure. Certainly "success" is not the goal, but coping with failure is a skill to be learned.

Pastoral ministry is open ended and never ending. I never have the sense that I have completed my work and thereby can take my ease. Any sense of success is a fleeting one at best. Often I have a sense of guilt over the work left undone. At times I have even felt overwhelmed by a sense of inadequacy and failure. For instance, I can preach two or three good sermons and feel extremely good then follow those up with sermons I think are awful. I have been through dozens of sequences like that.

Worse still is the following scenario. Someone will inform me that one of our members is in the hospital and has been there a whole week. I respond, "I never knew it," only to hear, "But I left a message on your machine." Somehow I did not get the message, or if I did, I forgot. One time I knew in advance someone was going to be operated on, I knew the date, time, and place. Still I let it get away from me. I wanted to pray with and be present with the individual, and, oh, does the guilt come flooding in.

It is not pleasant to preach bad sermons. I have preached some awful sermons, real stinkers! There have been more than a few Sunday evenings when the notion of quitting crossed my mind. Most pastors feel like they want to quit once in a while.

Though this may embarrass me later, but for the sake of others who might be like me, I do admit to having walked out of a couple of church council meetings saying, "I am out of here." I have done it. I hate to admit it, but I have done it. It occurred at times when I was very low, after having preached four or five poor sermons in a row and had a person or two leave the church. I felt like I was failing in my ministry. In one instance, I had found out that so-and-so was going to leave the church, and one of my closest partners in the church had attacked me in public. Suddenly there it was: "I am out of here! I am not subjecting my family and myself to this anymore!"

However, a pastor can not easily walk off and leave a church. Though there may be a certain number of people in the congregation who are against a pastor, there are others who are supportive and appreciative. A pastor must be careful about declarations of resignation, let me tell you. There will be times when a sense of inadequacy is strong and there are prolonged streaks where nothing seems to go well—do not be surprised or easily shaken. I do not say these things to discourage, but to encourage. Pastors who feel unique in their experience are the most vulnerable to discouragement and error. It is better to know how it really is. And, we must remember that we endure all things in order to preach the free grace of Jesus Christ.

If the pastor has a family, there will be people who will attack it. If the pastor has a dog, the dog may be maligned. Who knows? Once there is a "dragon" in the congregation, the whole family is open for attack. I am amazed at what some of "God's people" will do to and say about the pastor's family.

James Chuck, forty years the pastor of the First Chinese Baptist Church of San Francisco, tells the story of a young seminarian's disappointment in the progress of his first pastorate. He found many of the people in the church to be less than faithful. Dr. Chuck's response—"We've known about this phenomenon for some time."

The very people we count on will suffer a lack of faith, often at critical junctures in the life of the church. And when one person's faith slips, it is not unusual for it to turn into a kind of epidemic. What a disappointment it can be, especially in the small church where a little ripple makes a large wave.

It is this sort of thing, maybe more than anything else that has caused me pain and distress. Just when it seems we are being blessed by some growth, a key member or two will suddenly disappear. Week after week will go by and it begins to appear that they have left the church. And when I reach out to them, they avoid me. This does not go unnoticed, of course, and people began to ask, "Where is so and so?"

My tendency is to blame myself. If only I had kept in better contact, or, If only I could make people more excited about coming to church, or, If only I could preach better, or, If only, so on and so on. Usually the problem is more akin to a personal faith crisis on the part of the person or some kind of family or job problem that causes a person to want to hunker down at home on Sunday morning. But I tend to assume the worst. Certainly, sometimes my fears are well grounded.

This, however, is the ordinary flow of ministry; I am never very far away from it happening to me—a couple of weeks or more, at best. Despite every effort, I know now that it goes with the territory.

Probably the greatest sense of guilt comes from my seeming failure to add numbers to the church. Someone recently said to me, "Kent, how come the church is getting smaller?" I had to spend a lengthy period of time explaining, and before it was over we began to see that, in fact, the church was growing a little after all. However, it was a very unpleasant time. It took forty-five minutes to present the reason for the tact I was taking. Afterwards, tired and frustrated, my feelings got the better of me and I felt low for several days. It is at times such as this when I have to be clear about whom I am serving and why.

Pastors are tempted to quit as I spoke of earlier, and sometimes they actually do quit.

A pastor may be forced to resign. Pastors may realize the church ministry is hazardous to their health, even potentially deadly. If so, it may be time to get out. I have seen a number of ministers literally lose their health, their sanity, and almost lose their relationship with God because of what they experienced in a local church. It is not the end of the world to resign from a church, but I would do it very carefully, not suddenly. If necessary, take a week or two off. If that will not do it, take a short sabbatical (if possible). Find an experienced pastor to talk to; consult with someone from the denomination (if there is one). If leaving is the only choice, so be it. But do it in such a manner that a new pastor will not be sabotaged and the church family will not be damaged. Strive for dignity and calmness so that there is a fitting closure. Neither one pastor nor one church does the kingdom of God make. Yet, each pastor is precious in God's sight and each church belongs to the King.

Pastors who survive and flourish will learn to deal with the temptation to succumb to guilt and a sense of personal inadequacy. Ultimately our survival and health are based upon our relationship with Jesus. He is our righteousness, He is our strength, and we need not be superstar pastors to earn His love and acceptance.

Never give up!

☞ How do you react to failure?

☞ Have you ever been an unfaithful church member?

☞ Can you imagine a legitimate reason to resign from a church?

☞ Have you ever done so?

## Thirty-three

# Having A Trade

"What are you going to do now that you have resigned?" I asked.

"Landscape work, cutting grass, sprinkler systems—the kind of stuff I did while I was in seminary. I got more pleasure out of caring for the church grounds than I did pastoring the church. I'm glad I'm prepared for something anyhow."

✛    ✛    ✛    ✛    ✛

In a telephone company's Yellow Pages of the First Century AD Jesus would have been listed as a building contractor. A *tekton* in the Greek (see Mark 6:3), is a designation that can mean carpenter or maybe a stone mason or builder: Jesus worked with his hands. Probably He acquired some skills under the tutelage of an older and experienced *tekton*, Joseph. (see Mark 13:55)

Paul, skilled in the working of leather as were Priscilla and Aquila, periodically used his craft to meet his needs so that he would not be dependent upon others. He would, though, receive gifts from various churches and individuals from time to time but not as a regular habit.

At various times I have found it necessary to be able to make a living on my own without having to be dependent upon a church. However, I believe it is important for pastors to be dependent on those they minister to for their livelihood. When Jesus sent the disciples out two by two (see Luke 10) they were instructed to take no money with them, and they were to stay in the house in which they first entered. From this an important principle may be derived: ministers, pastors particularly, are to be reliant upon the churches in which they minister. Certainly, the "worker deserves his wages" (Luke 10:7)

Yet I think it is important for pastors to have the capacity to support themselves and their families outside of the church if need be. I have seen tragic circumstances arise when this was not the case. When pastors, usually with families, are dismissed, forced to resign, or must preside over the closing of a church and no immediate ministry is available, they may have little or no financial resource. It can be a damaging experience, especially for children. Years spent in Bible college and seminary do not usually result in the acquisition of marketable skills. In short, it is not always easy for an ex-pastor to find a job.

If I were dismissed here, or be forced to quit, I would want to be able to provide for my family. I am not going to reveal details here, but I have a couple of means by which I am able to do this. Having an assurance that God will care for us, perhaps care for us through a job skill, is consistent with scriptural principles.

Having a way of making a living and supporting a family will allow pastors stand their ground with some strength and courage in the event of a crisis. A pastor might stay in a desperate, even dangerous situation, due to a fear of not being able to survive. It is not that a pastor develops an arrogant or independent attitude: those attitudes do not become the servant of God. The servant is submissive to the *Head of the Church*, and to the church itself. The preacher submits to the ministry; however, it does not mean submission to a person, a group, or a church that would attempt to exercise ungodly power. This circumstance does come up from time to time. It has happened to me. It may happen again.

The kinds of trades or job skills one might engage in are many and varied. The construction trades, building, painting, landscaping, plumbing, electrical, masonry, and so forth, these are skills where jobs can usually be found. And, of course, computer skills may prove valuable. But whatever it might be, I suggest that pastors have the ability to perform some labor or service that would allow them to take care of themselves and their families if necessary.

☞ Do you have a trade or job skill that could see you through a difficult time?

☞ Are there steps you might take to acquire one?

☞ Does my suggestion seem biblically sound or not?

## Thirty-four

# Own a Pickup Truck!

"Nice truck, man." Actually his truck looked about as bad as mine.

"Thanks. The odometer has turned over twice and yet there has been absolutely no repair work done to the transmission or engine. Ugly, but I love it."

"You've got to be the only preacher I know who would drive his truck to a funeral."

✢ ✢ ✢ ✢ ✢

Own a pickup truck! The reader asks, "Is this guy serious?" Yes, I am; in fact, I would not be without one.

If I were the president of a seminary I might consider a requirement that no one would graduate unless they owned a pickup truck. That comment might seem somewhat odd, but there is a serious point to this.

I usually have a fairly old one and I am partial to Fords. Presently I have a newer one (only 10 years old), but I favor an old truck I do not mind seeing it dented up when I loan it out. There are so many times when a pickup is needed and it is not so easy to rent or borrow one. Own a pickup truck!

Get a big one, not one of those little ones. Get a big V-8 with an 8-foot bed. It does not matter how it looks. They are fairly cheap.

I use mine primarily to help people move. Anyone who has had to make a major move when money was tight knows what a traumatic event moving can be. Moving is usually a most stressful time, comparable to any significant loss. Pastors help people through the death of a loved one and divorce, yet moving is often neglected. Moving may be the result of a divorce. It may be necessitated because of an economic down turn, loss of a job, a debilitating illness, retirement, or some other unhappy reason.

Without exaggeration, which means I am not going to use preacher license, I have helped several hundred people move over the three decades of my pastoral ministry. On top of that are the small moves, little jobs that come up frequently (at least once a month) like moving a couch, a refrigerator, washer or dryer, a bed, a chest of drawers. These moves are not easily done without a pickup truck. This very day I loaded up and unloaded a cord of firewood. So many people are completely stymied when it comes to a move, and what a wonderful service it can be to help someone load up their stuff and move it for them.

My aim is to make a move a fun event. Some of us at Miller Avenue routinely gather together for them. And we are pretty efficient at it. We can save somebody hundreds, sometimes thousands of dollars, simply through the use of an old pickup truck.

It is a wonderful service. I think it is one of the most important and significant ministries that a pastor can possibly do in the actual ongoing life of a church. People move. And it is such a great thing to be able to help somebody move, help relieve them of that pressure and anxiety.

For many years I had a 1972 Ford pickup truck. I bought it in 1978 for $1500.00. I sold it for $500.00 recently. And that thing was worth its weight in gold. Before that I had a 1955 Ford pickup truck and it was an ugly beast, but it sure did a lot of good work. Now I have a 1991 Ford 3/4-ton pickup truck, and that thing does a ton of work.

If I were the president of a seminary I would probably let somebody graduate if they did not own a pickup truck. Probably!

☞ Pickup trucks may not appeal to you. You don't really have to have one.

☞ Do you have any ideas for some thing or some means that might work as a substitute to having a pickup?

Thirty-five

# Weddings and Funerals

"I have to tell you this is not my first time. Well, it is my third. But we are worried about something. What denomination are you?"

"American Baptist," I answered.

"We used to be Catholic. What happens then?"

"Well, if I did the ceremony that would make you Methodists."

✢　✢　✢　✢　✢

Weddings and funerals have presented me with excellent opportunities to present the gospel, and have, in fact, generally expanded my pastoral ministry.

Weddings are not necessarily easily done. I have six or seven wedding ceremonies that cover most situations.* It is irrelevant to me whether people have a church or religious background or not. (On this subject I may seem to be hopelessly liberal, but I have adopted this approach so that I can present the gospel to people I might not otherwise encounter.)

Furthermore, I do not require premarital classes though I know most ministers will. Because of the high divorce rate some are calling for a renewed emphasis for premarital counseling as though this would be the great cure. It does not seem so to me, but I think premarital classes and counseling may be helpful.

It is enough that a couple wants to be married; my view is that adults understand what they are doing and do not need me involved in the process. If requested, I will discuss pertinent issues. Few couples want to.

When I ran the Marin Christian Counseling Center I would not marry anyone unless they went through a six-week premarital session with me. I soon discovered that people would not be honest about themselves or their relationship out of fear I would disapprove or attempt to interfere. In the fifth week I would ask, "How do you fight?" I wanted to get at a couple's strategy for conflict resolution. Invariably the response was, "We don't fight." I figured this had to be a lie. As a result, I began to question the value of my premarital counseling. And the truth is I am not trained to be a marriage counselor.

Couples I marry do not have to be attendees of Miller Avenue. The same holds true for a funeral. I will accept almost any wedding or funeral that comes my way. However, I will not perform the so called "sacred unions"; I will not join homosexuals, and I will not perform phony ceremonies for people (men and women) who are living together and merely want their union "blessed", so-called, without the legal formality. But I will marry anyone who can be legally married and where there is nothing theologically or morally questionable in the ceremony. And I do this service to the best of my ability.

The primary ministry to the people I marry occurs when I send out a sermon tape to acknowledge anniversaries. It has proven to be a good way to present the gospel. To many of the people I perform weddings for I become their pastor. When the normal crises of life occur, I may get a phone call. Some wonderful things have happened. Without exaggeration, the most fruitful evangelism I engage in occurs in and around weddings.

When I do a wedding I do not preach at it. I do not say anything in the wedding other than what the couple wants me to say. The wedding is not the place to preach the gospel. A wedding is a wedding; it is not appropriate to take advantage of that circumstance.

It is the same with a funeral; I do not present the gospel unless I am specifically invited to do that. I will make certain statements and make myself available as best I can. Before the funeral or after the funeral I have a chance to personally present the gospel, but I will not take advantage of the circumstances. I am there to perform a particular function and I carry that out in the most dignified and helpful way I can.

On my computer I have different funeral ceremonies or orders of service and all I usually do is fill in the blanks. In addition, I have a number of bulletin covers available that are suitable for a funeral. There is never much lead-time for funerals; in fact, I have been called in the morning to do a funeral that afternoon.

When I receive a call for a funeral my first objective is to meet with the people who have experienced the loss. In that meeting I negotiate the contents of the bulletin that I will prepare for the memorial or funeral service. I hope to build rapport, I want people to feel comfortable with me. A week for so after the service, I may contact the principle people by mail or phone and offer to visit them. Additionally, I will contact them again on the anniversary of the death. Usually a grieving person has sufficient support early on, but that support diminishes over time. Being aware of this, I will make contact later on.

Weddings and funerals are rather stressful, especially the weddings. I've made some rather glaring errors at weddings. One of the worst occurred when I asked the bride, "Do you Suzy, take Joe, to be your wedded wife?" Once I presided at a wedding where hundreds of the cream of Marin society turned up. I couldn't calm down for two days afterward.

People often want to know if they can give money and I say "Yes." It is not helpful to be shy at that point. Name a figure and say, "Thank you." Put the money in the offering plate or put it away for fun family outings.

☞ Imagine the worst that could go wrong at a wedding or a funeral?

☞ Whatever you thought of could easily happen to you one day?

☞ If you were invited to present the gospel at a funeral, how would you go about it?

*I have wedding ceremonies and funeral services on file in my computer that I will be glad to e-mail to anyone who wants them.

Thirty-six

# Do Not Ask

"We have five hundred families in our church. How about you Pastor Philpott?"

"Somewhat less than that, probably about 95% less. And all our 'families' are not configured along the lines of the traditional model. We are small and blessed."

✛    ✛    ✛    ✛    ✛

The chapter's thesis: Do not ask other pastors about the size of their congregations or budgets. Miller Avenue is a small congregation. We vary in size from 30 to 60 people; there have been services when only 15 have attended. Pastors who preach conversion-oriented sermons may experience rather large fluctuations in the numbers of people who attend the public worship service. If someone began to preach strong gospel sermons to a congregation that had not heard such preaching, over time, a good percentage of that congregation would leave. No church would ever want to call me as a pastor when there was some question as to whether or not most of the congregation had actually experienced true conversion. If I were to go to such a church, maybe as high as 50% of the congregation would eventually leave. There would, hopefully, be people who would become converted, but those who realized they were not converted, and did not want to be, would leave.

Some would become angry with me for preaching such sermons. Some would want to hear "how to" sermons, sermons with folksy stories and humor, messages that would encourage, uplift, and inspire them. Some would find a more "user-friendly" church that would help them feel spiritual. Perhaps this evaluation is extreme, but such a scenario could well develop.

I was shaken, frankly, some years ago when I came to the realization that some people at Miller Avenue might be unconverted. I had been reading about the great awakenings in America, particularly the First Great Awakening, and became aware of the danger of false conversion. I often preach conversion-oriented sermons so that unconverted people might come to Jesus for salvation. Though I have always considered myself to be an evangelistic preacher, the fact is I did not preach much of the gospel to my own congregation; I assumed these people were genuinely born again. At first, I thought we might lose 20 percent. We lost at least 50 percent over the course of about a year and a half to two years. As church attendance began to decline people would say, "What happened to so-and-so, and how come we are not having a lot of people come?" These questions can be troubling, painful questions, and there can be a tendency to take it personally. Of course, I had an idea of the general dynamics and I would try to relate that, but many people found it hard to understand. The Holy Spirit will convict people of sin and they will become uncomfortable even angry. The fact is they can simply avoid the uncomfortable feelings by going to another church or drop out altogether.

It takes a certain amount of courage to withstand the pressure. At one point I nearly backed down. Dear members of the church would say, "Kent, we wish you would preach something else for a change." And so I would preach something else for a change, but that did not make much difference. Perhaps it was too late.

Other ministers heard about the shrinking Miller Avenue. A former Miller Avenue member or two would eventually tell the tale. In a week or two I would hear the result. "You know minister so-and-so doesn't agree with you." At the local ministerial meeting I would be asked, "Well, Kent how is the church going? How many people are attending now?"

I would think to myself, "Oh, I am failing. I am not being successful; other churches are growing and my church is getting smaller." It is an unpleasant feeling at minimum; however, it is something a pastor must come to terms with. At this point I have come to a place of acceptance, and it does not bother me as much any more. But, at least, I learned the inappropriateness of asking another pastor about attendance and budget.

Pastors can get into a kind of gamesmanship—the one who has the largest congregation and the biggest budget is the one who is winning. Everyone wants to know what the bottom line is. In the business world one might hear: "How many vice presidents do you have? What was your net last year?" "Which direction are you sales headed in?" "What are your stock options worth now?" These measurements are, of course, deceiving. In addition, in my estimation, the assumptions are false; the size of the congregation and budget are *not* indicators of how well a pastor is doing. The very reverse may actually be the truth.

We are beginning to see the outcome of the "church growth movement". When advanced and sophisticated tele-marketing techniques were applied to church growth, churches grew like crazy, staff members were added, budgets went through the roof, property was purchased, buildings went up, and people were filling up the pews. Phenomenal rates of growth were reported and everyone wanted in on it. Absolutely staggering!

The "unchurched" were attracted to the "user friendly," seeker churches, attracted more to the church, often, than to Jesus and His cross. In addition, the unconverted do not stay very long—they are soon off looking for the next exciting thing. And unconverted people do not give much money and will renege on their capital funds campaign pledge. When it gets down to it, they are not committed servants of Jesus. They want to be fed. They want to be cared for. They want to be inspired and excited. They want attention given to them. After a while that must break down and they will go away. Now the capital funds campaign begins to falter, the construction on the new building is going to have to be reexamined and maybe even terminated. Staff is going to have to be let go. The finance committee is thrown into one desperate meeting right after another. It is no longer any fun to go to the church board meetings because the focus is now on downsizing. And this is happening all across America—sadly so.

We want to get away from thinking that bigger is better. My view is that bigger is not always better, and I am going to discuss this a little more in the chapters

"Pastoring the Small Church," and "Pastoring the Large Church."

I avoid asking a pastor, "How large is the church?" I am not going to ask another minister how large the budget is. It is none of my business in the first place.

These have been some rather "off the cuff" remarks. I hope I have not offended anybody unduly by this, but I think there is something serious here—we do not gauge our value or that of anyone else on the basis of *the size of a congregation* or *a budget*. We are called to be faithful servants of our Lord Jesus Christ, and that alone matters. What I hope for more then anything else is to hear Jesus say, "Well done, good and faithful servant!" That must be enough for me.

✠   ✠   ✠   ✠   ✠

 The best case of all: large numbers of people being both converted and faithful in their giving. Still, is it necessary to know the details?

☞ If the details are offered, or if we offer them, how may this be done so as to honor and glorify God and not the church and pastor?

Thirty-seven

# Our Need for a Confessor or Mentor

"Kent, I hear you are having trouble at home. I want you to know we are all praying for you."

This revelation came from a member of the congregation as I sat with my daughters and several of their friends prior to the beginning of our Sunday morning worship service.

"Thank you." I replied. "Did you hear I was having a problem?"

"Yes, that is what everyone is saying."

The only person I spoke to was one of the associate pastors. Yes, one daughter's behavior was disturbing me, and I had asked for strict confidence.

I felt greatly comforted.

✣　✣　✣　✣　✣

Some years ago spiritual advisors or directors were in vogue. This person might also function as a "confessor," that is, someone who could be trusted with the deep, dark secrets and sins. Twelve Step programs sometimes utilize such advisors, as do other programs in seminaries and Bible colleges. Throughout much of the history of the church there have been confessors.

The Scripture itself teaches us to confess our sins to one another. (James 5:16) Though we do not know much about how this operated in the early church, it would yet be a larger part of church life and practice, no doubt, if there were confessors who could be trusted to keep confidence.

A discreet person who can be trusted is not easy to find, and must be chosen, if sought for at all, with great care.

I have trusted friends and colleagues with certain things only to discover they were not able to hold the confidence. People in general, I believe, have a hard time keeping confidence. We want to be depended upon with all our heart and soul, but we sometimes fail. Many distressed pastors have compounded their problems by confessing their sins and other problems to colleagues, associates, or even members of the church.

Of course, I know it is helpful to have another human being to talk to, one who is empathetic and caring, and will not give advice or make suggestions. If an individual's spouse can be a reliable soul mate, so much the better. However, not all pastors are married, and not all spouses would even want or be able to serve as a confessor. There are things about pastoral ministry that are not easily shared with anybody.

Perhaps it is best if our Father in heaven were our confessor. He keeps perfect confidence and can be relied upon to forgive and comfort us in our innermost being.

A mentor, on the other hand, may be a valuable asset, especially for a "young" pastor. Having someone to learn from and be held accountable to could make the difference between joy and despair in the pastoral ministry. Such mentoring may be conducted on a formal basis, but usually it is on an informal basis.

Some people I consider to be mentors have been long dead, George Whitfield, Ashael Nettleton, Jonathan Edwards, and Martyn Lloyd-Jones among others. Over the years Charles Hadden Spurgeon has proven to be my favorite. (For those who are online, at the locator type in SEARCH.SPURGEON.) Through their books, sermons, and other writings, they have become people I look to in terms of experience, theology, and the manner in which they conducted their ministry.

Pastors will serve as confessor or mentor for others, sometimes without realizing the exact nature of the relationship, and perhaps it is best that they occur in the natural and normal flow of life and ministry. I particularly welcome the mentoring relationship though I wonder if I am wise enough to so serve. I do not particularly welcome the confessor relationship and I doubt that I will allow any such arrangement on a formal basis.

I have my mentors, some are living, some are dead, and one is risen from the dead. I have both a confessor and a mentor who is seated at the right hand of the throne of God who intercedes for me. Perhaps this will be sufficient.

☞ At this point in your life, would you prefer having a mentor or serving as one?

☞ Is there anyone in your life that would fit?

Thirty-eight

# Thoughts on Retirement

"Do you think the social security system will collapse?"

"No, it will probably be there for us, but it may not be enough."

"Well, do you look forward to retirement then Kent?"

"I may not be able to pastor and preach always, but I will, God willing, never retire from serving the Lord."

✛  ✛  ✛  ✛  ✛

I often ask myself the question, "What am I doing here?" And thankfully, the answer becomes clearer as the years go by. Basically I do one thing and that is point people to Jesus, whether they are Christians or not. In my sermons, in the Bible studies I teach, in my conversation, and counsel, I point people to Jesus. And I can do this all of my life; I do not have to be a pastor to do so.

But I love the pastoral ministry precisely because it gives me continual opportunities to say, "Look to Jesus and be saved." I am aware I have greater potential for pointing to Jesus than most other members of Miller Avenue. Therefore I am jealous of my ministry.

So then, I will never retire as long as I have breath and strength to point others to Jesus. However, I must plan for retirement financially. And this is often difficult for the pastor of a small church.

I am aware that Miller Avenue must have a pastor who can carry out the work and that will mean, sooner than later, a younger person than myself. I can see myself in a "pastor emeritus" status. This may not be possible until I begin to retire and release funds for another pastor, but I will not be able to do that unless there is money for me to retire on and social security may not, almost certainly will not, be enough.

What to do? At least, $2000 should be set aside each year for an Individual Retirement Account—the IRA. Notice I said "at least." Pastors are eligible for a 403B retirement plan that allows for more than $2000 to go into a retirement account. The maximum amount is about 16% of the total salary.

Some pastors will respond, "I would if I could." And I understand. At the same time, please allow me to strongly urge the IRA yearly contribution. It amounts to $167 a month. I know that for the small church pastor this represents a sizeable chunk of money. If $167 is unrealistic, then pick a number and be consistent about it. Perhaps have whatever investment company you go with take the money directly out of your bank account.

It is important for a church to know their pastor will be secure in retirement and is making the necessary arrangements.

Young people beware; there will come a time when even you will realize the work is more than you can get done. Plan now for retirement, but know that you will never really retire.

✢    ✢    ✢    ✢    ✢

☞ Are you putting money away for retirement?

☞ Have you ever talked to an investment advisor, perhaps one in your denomination?

☞ If you answer no to these questions maybe it is wise to consider your mortality and limitations.

Thirty-nine

# Pastoring the Small Church

"Pastor, how can we get more people into our church? We don't even have enough kids to run a Sunday school."

"I know what you mean. Even if we had seven or eight kids we could make a start. Plus we could use a new tenor and bass in the choir."

"So Kent, what are you going to do about it?"

"I wish I knew what to do. It seems we have tried a lot of things. I guess we are going to have to be faithful to do what we can and depend on the Lord to do the rest. But small or not, this is our church and I love the people God has already brought in."

It has been my privilege to pastor three churches. One, a small church—my first church when I was a seminary student—the Excelsior Baptist Church in Byron, California, is now closed. There were less than ten people the first Sunday in Byron and one Easter Sunday we almost reached capacity, fifty people. Attendance fluctuated over the two and a half years of my ministry there; twenty would be a good crowd. And on some Sunday evenings no one came at all.

174

One particular Sunday evening service comes to mind. Byron is a farming community in California's Central Valley, and summer temperatures would reach 100° or better. Attendance at the morning service was small as the temperature hit 90 by 10 AM. My daughters, Dory and Grace, aged eight and six, and I had made the 75-mile trip from Mill Valley alone since my wife had to work. We were obliged to spend the afternoon as best we could hoping to keep cool in the shade of trees at the local park. At 6 that evening the girls and I opened up the building, and first thing I cranked up the old swamp cooler. The temperature stood at 105°, but inside it was hotter still. From six to seven I studied my sermon, selected hymns, and tried to help the girls survive the heat and boredom. At seven we were still alone. I anticipated that no one would come to the service, but it was my job to be there. At five minutes past seven we sang a hymn, I preached the sermon, the three of us sang another hymn and then we had a closing prayer. At half past the hour I turned off the swamp cooler and we headed home.

The second church, considerably larger than the first, had two services Sunday morning and we would average 375 in attendance. I served as senior pastor and there were four associate pastors. In addition, we had a full time secretary and treasurer.

The third church, and hopefully my last, Miller Avenue, is a small church. Not that I purposely want it to be small; my intent is for the church to grow and I make every effort in that direction. But, the growth must come as a result of preaching for conversion and helping people grow up into the stature of the fullness of Jesus. I try to be careful not to act in such a way or implement programs designed to keep the church small. But this church is likely to remain small. Ours is a rather small building, we have no parking lot, only street parking and this is limited. Mill Valley is said to be the capital of the "New Age Movement" and few people, around 3% of the population, even attend church on Easter Sunday.

My hope is that people will be attracted to our church and we welcome all comers. We want to see the church grow. If it grows we will bless God for that, and if the church does not grow, we will bless God for that as well.

At Miller Avenue I do a lot of extra things that a pastor of a larger church might not. For instance, I do a considerable amount of janitorial work; I maintain the grounds including cutting the lawns. I do electrical work, painting, plumbing, carpentry, landscaping, and anything and everything else that needs to be done that I can figure out how to do.

Much of my four years of military duty was spent doing janitorial work though I was trained to be a medic. I could not have asked for better preparation for being the pastor of Miller Avenue. Sometimes I think that if I were president of a seminary (or dean of a seminary), in addition to the requirement of owning a pickup truck, there would be courses that taught building construction, electrical work, plumbing, janitoring, landscaping, roofing, painting, and the replacing of broken windows. At least there would be a couple of courses on practical handiwork since the small church pastor will be doing so much of it. And this is another reason why pastors must keep fit, healthy, and strong.

I make an effort that our faithful people do not feel bad for having a small church. For instance, I avoid pointing out how few there are of us, and I do not blame the people for the fact that we do not have a larger church. We appreciate the fellowship we have with each other; we see ourselves as partners in ministry. And we preach the gospel just as intently and earnestly for 30 people as we would for 300 people or 3,000 people.

It amazes me how many ministries even a very small church can undertake. Our budget hovers around $70,000 a year, and yet we have a worldwide ministry. We conduct, I believe, significant ministry in regard to our divorce recovery and parenting workshops. We do jail ministries (a rather significant jail ministry, actually). We have a wonderful gospel choir; I sing in it, too. We have a television ministry that reaches most of our Marin County as well as all of San Francisco, and a Saturday lunch for those in need. Through our tithes and offerings we encourage and participate in ministries all over the world. We have a website that has the potential of reaching around the globe. There is an audiotape ministry. We have an inexpensive tape duplicator and for a very small amount of money a month we send sermon tapes all over, now even around the world. It is not necessary to be a large church to have a significant ministry.

We sing the great hymns of the church, we sing modern choruses, and we sing songs that people in the church have written. We preach the gospel, teach the Bible, and we have a Sunday school—a very small Sunday school. We baptize people, dedicate children, marry and bury people—all the ministries that churches traditionally do.

The small church is precious to me as a pastor. Many learn it is a blessing and a privilege to pastor a small church.

☞ How important is the size of a church to you?

☞ Can you preach with "heat" to a small church or do you need a lot of people in the congregation to inspire you? Don't answer so quickly, giving the expected answer. Think about it.

## Forty

# Pastoring the Large Church

"Kent, we have so many people now I hardly know any of them. There isn't enough Sunday school space and the choir director wants a raise in salary. What are we going to do about it?"

"I wish I knew. We can't very well send people away or make it impossible for new people to come either. And money wise, the demands grow more quickly than the supply."

"You remember Kent, how great it was in the early days when we had just that small committed core of people. Sure I like being a big church, but we are losing something, too."

This brief chapter is not intended to be a definitive discussion of the complex process of pastoring a large church. Rather, there follows some simple observations, with some bias, about being pastor of a large church.

By "large" I mean anything over 100 people. By my reckoning, a small church is 100 or under. Large churches are 100 and over because at that point more than one pastor is generally needed. Based on my experience one pastor can care for maybe 75 people and 100 is a stretch. At Miller Avenue we have a music director/choir director (that is one person) and another part-time staff person who teaches and preaches. I preach three out of four Sundays now but for years I did almost all the preaching. And I like to have other people preach. I do not do so well preaching every single Sunday month after month. I need a little rest from it, not physically so much, but I need to be sure that I am preaching sermons that are of value.

A large church usually results in the pastor being head of a staff, and it is here where most of the problems arise. Looking back on pastoring a larger church I recall that too much of my time was preoccupied with caring for the problems generated by the associate pastors and other staff members. A reader might imagine I may be overstating it, or maybe that my policies or administration techniques were the real problem; and maybe its true. Maybe my personality and gifts are better suited to pastoring the smaller church. I am a bit of a "type-A" personality; that is, I am a hard worker. I set a high standard in terms of expectations. I do not tolerate slothfulness; I admit it. No doubt I created many of my own problems when I pastored a church with a multiple staff.

I am not against the large church. A church will often grow to fit the circumstances. The size and makeup of a community, the capacity of both the building and pastor, the expectations, needs, and goals of a congregation and many other factors will influence the size of a congregation. The larger church has its own problems, and it becomes a major responsibility simply to administrate it.

I am not an eight-to-fiver. Generally I arrive at my office at 9 AM and by noon I am gone and will not return until late in the afternoon. During that period no one is around. I can get away with that. There is an answering machine and I am careful to make callbacks. In a larger church, however, the pastor is pretty much tied to the office all day working with staff people. There must be meetings with the librarian, choir director, grounds people, Sunday school leaders, department heads, and so on. And, of course, the treasurer and the finance committee people are never far away. It goes on and on. So much of it is a diversion from the primary tasks of gospel preaching and Bible teaching. I think there is a limit to how much the gospel preacher can be involved in. Pastors can easily become misdirected and eventually worn down by caring for all of the "necessaries" that go with the large church.

We will have wonderful and fruitful large churches, and to whom much is given, much is required. I am increasingly in favor of the small church. If Miller Avenue got to be double or triple the size it is now, I think it would be time to start another church nearby. I doubt I would be able to cope with a large church again.

May the Lord bless the pastor of a large church with grace and strength so that the focus remains on gospel preaching and Bible teaching.

✣ ✣ ✣ ✣ ✣

You, dear reader, observed my bias. You say, "If you are faithful the church will grow." Probably so, all other things being equal as they say, but not as a strict matter of course.

☞ Suggestion: Defend my position and then argue against it.

Forty-one

# On Being an Associate

"What title should I use? Associate pastor?"
   "How about 'minister-at-large'?" I asked.
   "Kent, what are you saying?"
   "Well, you are bigger than I am. You definitely qualify as a large minister."

✣   ✣   ✣   ✣   ✣

Many, perhaps most, pastors are associates or assistants: youth pastor, senior pastor, couple's pastor, single's pastor, children's pastor—these are the more common designations. Most of the material in this book is directly applicable to associate or assistant pastors. But there are a few things I want to say specifically about being an associate or assistant pastor.

I served as an assistant. My title, "minister-at-large,"* meant I had a wide range of responsibilities. I lead worship, taught a Sunday school class, preached occasionally, and did anything else the senior pastor requested. After a personal crisis that had me thinking of leaving the ministry, being on a pastoral staff gave me an opportunity to rebuild. That time proved to be a valuable experience, one I am very thankful for. Before, I had been either the only pastor or the senior pastor. As a senior pastor, with assistant pastors, I learned a little about the special circumstances of the associate or assistant pastor.

Of first importance let me say that the survivors in pastoral ministry are those who have a compelling desire to be a servant of Jesus. Those who are hungry for power and authority may actually attain it, but generally will not hold it for long.

Allow me to invoke, again, one of my favorite allusions, that of a baseball team. Of course I know that the metaphor of a team does not perfectly apply to a church's multiple pastoral staff, but there are enough similarities for the metaphor to be an acceptable allusion.

Whatever the title might be—associate, assistant, minister at large—staff members must recognize they are members of a team. To be effective a team must work in close cooperation and be mutually supportive. Each member of the team must learn to submit to the others and to view others as better than themselves. I would like to stress that last point: *see others as better than themselves.* This is a biblical principle and an important one.

A team member is someone who roots for the other player, someone who is not quick to criticize when an error is made. A valued team member offers advice, council, and critique when it is asked for, and only then. Good team members are encouraging and supportive even when they feel they could do a better job. A good team member prays for the others and looks for opportunities to lift them up.

On a baseball team some players are equipped to be outfielders, some to be infielders, and some to be pitchers or catchers. Among the infielders there will be those who can play shortstop and those who can play first base; one will usually not excel at the other position. Some people have speed, some hit with power, while others are slap hitters (what we used to call *banjo hitters*), yet each one is important to the overall team. On the pitching staff are starters, relievers, and closers. They will all be needed at various stages of a game. I have seen teams where the pitchers began to compare themselves with one another and strive for individual recognition; the result is contention, bad feelings, and a losing record. A team with "bad chemistry," personality problems, is no fun to play on.

Staff ministers will usually have a specific area of responsibility. If it is to be the head of the Sunday school, that job must be done well. If it is to open the doors and greet the congregation, this deserves every effort. The principle is to be faithful in whatever job is assigned. Faithfulness in one area may lead, though not necessarily, to expanded opportunities for service. The associate must let others make any evaluations about job performance and especially be careful to avoid self-promotion and comparisons.

Associate and/or assistant pastors will generally begin to think that they can do a better job than the senior pastor. More specifically, they imagine they can preach, teach, and care for the congregation more effectively. This, in itself, is not so bad. In fact, it may be a necessary quality in a minister. It at least shows that there is a desire to do the work of a pastor. However, if such tendencies go unchecked, division in the church may be the result, or it can lead to jealousy, resentment, gossip, and finally rebellion. Players sitting on the bench, perhaps a role player such as a pinch-hitter, ought to think they are capable of being starters or every day players. But "bad chemistry" results if the player begins to moan and whine and undermine the other players. When I see it on one of my teams, I deal with it right away and if it continues will remove a troublesome player from the roster.

A staff minister must not allow people to give them money directly. It is not unknown for someone to say something like; "I do not feel good about some of the ministry of the church. I disagree with the church budget. I would like my tithe to go to you." This is rather commonplace and it is hard to resist for many reasons. But to accept money directly is a mistake and must never be allowed. No money should ever be received except that which goes through the general church fund with the knowledge and approval of the church council.

Pastors who lead small groups such as a Bible study, fellowship group, prayer circle, and so forth, may unwittingly develop fans or followers who are overly devoted to them. A leader who has a bit of a critical attitude will have a tendency to attract people who are somewhat rebellious or immature. A situation can develop where there is a group within a group—a sub-church. It is like the baby porcupine playing with the balloon. Mama porcupine says to papa porcupine, "This won't last long." The sub-group will not last long either, however spiritual and however many prophecies and visions have been given in order to support the legitimacy of the subgroup; it will not last long but will cause many to stumble in their faith. Associates must be careful they not do anything that would upset the overall well-being of the larger church.

My dad always enjoyed being an usher; he delights in being a doorkeeper. He finds pleasure and joy in simple service to Jesus. This is the attitude the associate should have. The salary, if there is one, the recognition, if there is any, is not the goal. God's glory is goal enough. Having a place to serve and an opportunity to "wash the feet of the saints" in the name of Jesus, this is the prize. As the Psalmist said, "I would rather be a doorkeeper in the house of my God than dwell in the tents of the wicked" (Psalm 84:10). For those of us who have at one time or another lost their ministry these words ring so very true. To serve Jesus, to preach the gospel, to bring glory to God—these and these alone are to be valued above all else.

☦   ☦   ☦   ☦   ☦

☞ What advantages are there to being an associate as opposed to being either the single or senior pastor?

☞ If you had your druthers, what position of service would you prefer?

---

*Any position with the title "pastor" generally requires a congregational vote in most churches. So that I do not force the congregation to call another pastor I use the term, "minister at large". Generally associates and assistants are brought in by a senior pastor, and generally leave, or at least offer their resignation, if that senior pastor leaves for whatever reason. Situations vary, but in general at least, this has been my experience.

Forty-two

# Love Your Spouse

"I wish you treated me as well as you do the people in the church."

"You mean I don't?"

"Sometimes you have more patience and understanding for the craziest person in the church than you have for me."

"Hmm, I am going to have to think about that one."

Ministers, particularly preachers and teachers, are very used to speaking and may not be good listeners. Listening is an art to be learned, and for the pastor, listening to the person we are married to, if we are in fact married, is vital.

The ministry is extraordinarily stressful. Imagine what my wife is faced with. For one, she must get along with a whole host of people, most of whom she did not choose to be involved with. In our small church most everyone is easy to get along with and many have become good friends. In a larger church it might not necessarily go so well.

Often-times the spouse of a pastor may be a target for certain "dragons" (see chapter 44) in the church.

Of course, there are many expectations placed upon the spouse. Sometimes the spouse is seen as an employee of the church, in fact, the minister may be looked at in the same way. Of course, this is a faulty concept, but people who view the pastor as an employee may perceive the spouse as an employee as well. And they may be treated as such, even evaluated on the basis of their performance; the spouse is likely to come up short.

Pastor's children will usually have exceptional expectations placed upon them; these may include responsibilities within the church as well as exemplary behavior. The parents will sense the pressure to perform more keenly than the children will, but it can be extremely uncomfortable and unpleasant for kids especially in their teen aged years.

The pastor's spouse is often placed in situations that may be very difficult. Many pastors are sociable and enjoy being with other people, but the pastor's spouse may not. It helps, of course, if the pastor's spouse is a welcoming, accepting, hospitable, merciful kind of individual, and these are traits that often are important for a pastor's spouse. However this is not always, nor necessarily must be, the case.

Pastors must love their spouse. The spouse must come first; the church cannot come first. The biblical model is that the family must come first. And pastors will find when they begin to lose their family they will begin to lose their ministry.

When a spouse is alienated, irritated, offended, or somehow in pain, ministry in the church simply will not function very well. It seems that a high percentage of the "little" squabbles (not fights, of course) my wife and I get into occur on Sunday morning. Not a few times it was all I could do to face the people and preach the sermon. Nothing takes the inspiration and power out of the preacher more than a family disturbance. I have known pastors who have feigned sickness rather than have to step into the pulpit after a fight with a spouse or child. It is positively disheartening and I mention it here to make it plain that these things do happen. In such a case it is necessary to carry on as best one can while remembering the words, "Never give up".

When there are problems within the family, sadly, most pastors will hide them from the congregation. It would be a rare church that would have the maturity and grace to support a pastor and family through difficult times.

☞ Is it apparent that if there is trouble at the pastor's home, ministry in the church will suffer?

☞ How is it so?

☞ What does loving one's spouse mean?

☞ How is it actually lived out?

## Forty-three

# Spend Time with Your Children

"'Spare the rod, spoil the child,' right?"

This was no question, it was a pronouncement. But I had a ready answer.

"Right, the shepherd's rod to guide and protect. Can you imagine the foolish shepherd beating his very own sheep with a rod? Some mistakenly think shepherds beat their sheep. Talk about not understanding the Word! The shepherd as parent, yes, I like that. Protecting, caring, feeding, being with... yes, a good and wise parent."

✤   ✤   ✤   ✤   ✤

From my first marriage I have three children, daughters Dory and Grace, and son Vernon. Dory and Grace have given me eight grandchildren and my son Vernon has recently married. There is no telling how many grandchildren I may end up with. But as I look back on the parenting of my three oldest children I realize I did not spend anywhere near enough time listening to them, talking with them, and being with them.

During the period of my children's early and teen years I was the young, up-and-coming pastor. Writing books, establishing churches, preaching and teaching, working with associate pastors, starting Bible studies and fellowship groups, involved in a doctorate program—working 80 to 90 hours a week, every week for years and years. And though that time was not completely wasted, I did not spend the kind of time with my kids that I should have. It is something I now regret. The old saying, "kids are grown up and gone before you know it," is a fact I can testify to.

Time spent with children is well spent. We use the term "bonding;" perhaps it is overused, but I think there is some truth in the concept. We connect with, bond with our children, as we spend time with them. There is a wonderful book by two New York social workers, Adele Faber and Elaine Mazlish. The book is titled *How To Talk So Kids Will Listen and Listen So Kids Will Talk*. (Avon Books, New York) The writers are not Christians, but it describes how parents can both learn to talk with and listen to their children. My wife and I continue to apply the book with my twin daughters, Laura and Jenna, who at the time of this writing are ten years old. Now I am learning to talk with and listen to them so they will want to talk with and listen to me.

As preachers and teachers we tend to be so preoccupied with talking that we do not often listen. When I am with a group of people, they are often expecting to hear what I have to say. They are asking questions, seeking information about some biblical passage, wanting help with some theological point; so I am generally geared to talking. Nothing wrong here, but if it carries over into every area of our life it can become problematic. If with our children, spouse, friends, neighbors, and people in the community in general we are constantly talking then we will not be hearing. And it is true with me that I tend to avoid people who are constantly presenting their point of view, people who are so narcissistic that conversation seems to always revolve around them.

On that familiar scale of one to ten, if ten is a good listener and one is not a good listener, I may be at a three or a four. But I am convinced I was at the one level for most of my life.

I learned some years ago to spend time with each of my girls separately. Perhaps I will take one of them to breakfast, or we will take a walk, go for a bicycle ride, or drive somewhere in the car. I take one of them with me when I am doing an errand, even though I could save time by doing it alone. Spending individual time with my girls is precious time and will, I believe, bring great reward.

☞ Do you consider yourself a good listener?

☞ Suggestion: question some people close to you on this point. And one more suggestion: intentionally engage a person, your own child if applicable, and focus on listening and keeping your own mouth shut. Examine yourself then; see how well you did.

Forty-four

# Dragons in the Church

"Kent, have you got a couple hours? I've got a real mess here." Seymour, pastor of a nearby church, of another denomination, sounded excited and disturbed.

"You want me to come over?"

"Thanks but no. I don't want anybody to know we talked. It involves you."

"Okay, now I'm interested. Is it about Ed?"

"That's it. How about I meet you at the high school football field?"

Ed had just left the church I pastored, mad and vengeful. His parting words to me went something like this: "You don't preach the Word. You are a hopeless liberal. You are a poor shepherd. You won't preach the truth because you're afraid you'll run off the big givers. I am leaving and I want my tithes for this year back." Ed had been a friend for ten years.

✧    ✧    ✧    ✧    ✧

Many years ago my friend and former pastor, and the long time pastor of Hillside Church of Marin, Prince Altom, gave me a book by Marshall Shelley titled, *Well-Intentioned Dragons* published by Word in 1985. The subtitle of the book is "Ministering to

Problem People in the Church." The dedication to that book is: "To those scorched by dragons but not reduced to ashes nor hardened beyond feeling, who in the face of beastliness maintain their humanity and divine calling this book is dedicated."

I recommend this book though it may now be out of print. It helped me realize there were people in the church, often very well intentioned people, who could make my life miserable. Unhappily, I, as any pastor will, have encountered many such dragons.

Battling the dragons, perhaps more than anything else, beats the pastor down. It can bring depression, discouragement, panic attacks, and the urge to quit.

Every born again member of the church has a fallen nature; each Christian is a sinner. We are aware there is sin in the world, but the wise and mature pastor must realize that there will be sin in the church as well.

Reinhold Niehbur, a German theologian who came to Detroit, Michigan after having fled Hitler's Nazis, defined sin as "the will to power" in *The Nature and Destiny of Man*. Niehbur taught that the fallen nature manifests itself in a grasping for power over people and events, even over nature and God. This hunger for power is often the motivation of the "dragon" though it always, or almost always, will be unconscious.

Many people lack significant meaning in their day-to-day routine, but the church presents an arena where they can experience and exert a measure of power and authority. A lust for power over people and events may be expressed through a personal attack against a pastor or another leader in the church, or it may be directed against a form or structure that exists in the church. There are so many ways disturbances can occur that it seems impossible to list them all. That attacks will come should be no surprise. The challenge is learning to cope with and survive the attacks of the dragons.

Let me say, too, that dragons can change. Dragons have made transitions, became teachable, submitted to discipline, and abided by the counsel of Scripture. Every war with a dragon is not lost; dragons need not be slain nor slay.

I hesitate, however, and am uncertain at this point, because I have not always dealt effectively with the dragons. This chapter is probably written ten years prematurely. With that caveat in mind, here are a few suggestions.

One, when a dragon strikes, react slowly; let some time go by before any response is made. Take time to pray about and think through the circumstances. Do as little as possible at the outset.

Two, keep close counsel. Relating the details of an attack to others within the church may simply serve to spread the flames.

Three, I especially advise no letter writing. I have written a few letters in my time, and, with rare exception, I have regretted it.

Four, things will often "blow over" without doing anything about the situation at all. Many problem people will take themselves right out of the church, sometimes with a few others in tow, but that is all right. We talk about "blessed subtractions."

Five, there is the potential of using the problem resolution process of Matthew 18. If the war with the dragon continues for some time, this is the way to go. However, the first step, the "one on one" meeting may already be obsolete in that other people have already become involved. It may be beyond the small group process, too. This has been my experience as I am sometimes the last to know that war has been declared.

It may be that the best that can be done is to lay the situation before the church's clearing house, the church council, or some other board. If the problem continues unabated, then it must come before the entire congregation.

To complicate matters, the person or persons acting the dragon may have a semblance of a valid argument. For instance, I love and value Sunday school, yet I have not been successful in putting one together. I have tried several times and failed each time and have been attacked for this, and consequently the attacker has a point. However, my worth as pastor is not based simply on my ability or inability to put together a Sunday school. There need not have been a war at all, but the lust for power and authority caused the escalation. (see James 4:1-2) If conditions are beyond the point of "agreeing to disagree," which is often the case, someone will leave the church.

I recall three or four people who left Miller Avenue in a less than amiable manner. Once I nearly left myself. And when I think of these people I am still troubled. I wish I could go back and redo, or undo, what I did. For better or worse I usually act and that is why now, with hindsight, I suggest doing as little as possible as the main battle strategy. With the exception where an individual is acting the dragon by preaching, teaching, or otherwise expounding false and dangerous doctrine, less is best.

I have rambled a bit here and this chapter overlaps some others, but I think it is worth it to recognize that there will be dragons and that we will be damaged. We will be struck blows. This is why we have the armor Paul describes in Ephesians 6. If the armor were not needed it would not be provided. There will be wars with the dragons and we are equipped to face them.

✢  ✢  ✢  ✢  ✢

☞ Have you ever been a "dragon" yourself?

☞ Can you recount an instance where you witnessed a dragon in action?

☞ What ought to be a pastor's attitude toward dragons?

Forty-five

# Know and Face Your Limitations

"You know what the great prophet Clint Eastwood said? It was a Dirty Harry movie I think and it went like this—'You have got to know your limitations.'"

"So Kent you take that for the inspired Word of God?"

"No, but it makes sense anyway. I know I have my limitations. How about you?"

✢   ✢   ✢   ✢   ✢

Sometimes pastors get in over their heads, get involved with situations that, if they were to continue, might well be fatal, literally. The purpose of this chapter is to give a person permission to say: "I have not been called to the pastoral ministry" or, "I am not called to pastor this church" or, "I have got to take some time away from the church and figure this out."

It is best to pastor a church for a long time. It takes years, maybe five or more years, before a pastor feels comfortable and confident. It took me ten years at Miller Avenue to come to that place. I may be a little slower then some, but nevertheless, I think it took at least ten years here. Going from church to church, a few years here and a few years there, is generally a futile exercise and may be irresponsible.

How is success or effectiveness in pastoral ministry measured? Probably it has little to do with "nickels and noses." These may be indicative of a fruitful pastoral ministry, but they may not. It is not a sure indicator at any rate. I prefer not to create any measuring sticks at all. What I have called successful ministry has dissolved more quickly than you, the reader, might imagine possible. I have a measure that, if pressed, I would apply—freedom to preach the free grace of the gospel. And, if I get to preach and a few people show up to hear it, I am fine. God's will, I believe, has not so much to do with where but what. Where, the church location, or the church itself, is not central; the "what", the freedom to preach Jesus, is central for me.

Over the course of the past few decades I have come across people who realized they should not be pastors. They may have mistaken the zeal that often accompanies conversion for a calling to be a pastor. Or, more often, someone else observed the zeal and energy of the young convert and concluded such a person ought to be a pastor. Then away the young or new convert goes, to seminary, and finally into the ministry. Following the "honeymoon" period most new ministers enjoy, the pastor wakes up and says, "Wait a minute, I really do not want to be a pastor. I want to do something else."

Leaving the pastoral ministry requires a great deal of courage. I am thinking of two former associates who left the pastoral ministry to study medicine and currently are medical doctors and practicing Christians. Whether pastoring, attending to the fellowship supplies, leading the singing, serving as a doorkeeper—

these make no difference. The issue is faithful service in the name of Jesus. We are called to love Jesus and to abide in Him; this is first and foremost.

Some step aside from the ministry in order to evaluate who they are and what they ought to do with their lives. Sometimes people who have had moral failures take a leave of absence that they might recover and rebuild. And then some have simply decided they want out. It takes courage to face our limitations.

☞ If you could, if you had your way, would you leave the ministry?

☞ This is not a question of being discouraged and feeling you want to quit the ministry, this issue is more basic than that. Or, can you access your limitations, accept them, and yet press on in the ministry?

# Forty-six

# Angry Pastors

"_____"

"What was that you said pastor?"

"Oh, I didn't know you were standing there. Sorry about that. I just received a very disturbing letter."

"I am shocked. I feel betrayed. I feel like I caught you. I don't know what to do about it. Well, I've got to go."

✢ ✢ ✢ ✢ ✢

A psychiatrist once said: "Pastors are the angriest people I know." I am not sure about the scientific accuracy of that statement, but I think there is some truth to it.

I have had a number of people leave the church in a very short period of time, sometimes for legitimate, understandable reasons, other times for reasons I thought might even be demonic. A number of times I experienced a strong feeling of loss, and anger followed close behind. This is neither right nor wrong, it is simply how it is. Anger will be there, and perhaps that is what the psychiatrist meant when he said that pastors were the angriest people he knew.

Anger is a natural human emotion; it is not sinful in and of itself. We recall that Paul said, "In your anger, do not sin: Do not let the sun go down while your are still angry" (Ephesians 4:26). Paul accepted as fact that Christians will be angry and that it is no sin; however, anger must be resolved before something worse, actual sin, comes out of it. Anger is also a normal stage of the human grief reaction. When there has been a loss there will be, must be, grieving. In fact, anger, a major stage of grief, lasts longer, usually, than any other.

Pastors experience one loss after another, and as a result, are constantly going through the grief process though few recognize it. Therefore, pastors will have anger. Let me briefly explain how this can be.

Change is a normal part of the life of a church. People are coming and going. Many stay for long periods but even these will eventually leave even if it is through death. Each time a person leaves the church family, there is a loss. And as I have said before, where there is loss there will be grief, and anger is a part of that.

As pastor, I get to know the members of our church family well, sometimes very well. I do not maintain an emotional distance from the people in our fellowship; I am part of the spiritual community. Strong bonds will develop over the course of many years. There will be births, deaths, weddings, illnesses, struggles—all the experiences of life and I am there with my people. So when one leaves, however it occurs, I have a loss. Can I expect anger to be part of that? "Yes."

Without difficulty I could name fifty people whom I still miss who left a church I pastored ten or twenty even thirty years ago. I do not know if there is any anger attached to those losses or not.

Someone may leave the church in order to enter the ministry. This is a good reason to leave. But, people will leave the church in unpleasant ways, too. They may have a need to blame somebody for their leaving and the most obvious person to blame is the pastor. There are any number of "reasons" to be offended, a point in a sermon or Bible study, a budget decision, an apparent social slight, even the way the pastor speaks or dresses. The exiting person will tell others why they are leaving and, of course, it will get back to the pastor.

The above has happened to me a hundred times or more, but it can get worse. One pastor related an incident whereby a friend of a newly exited member announced both the person's departure and complaint in a public prayer. It was all quite spiritual. "Please bless so and so who had to leave because they could not get along with the pastor. Amen."

An "offense" may be imagined or real. (Some people are very easily offended.) But the pastor experiences loss anyway. When a person leaves a church for a legitimate reason there may be a process that helps bring closure to the departure. A "good bye" ceremony, celebration or some other form of acknowledgment may occur that serves to focus on the loss and allow for some grieving. When someone leaves the church for an unpleasant reason, there is no closure at all, nothing but a wound and eventually a scar.

Oddly enough it has often turned out that the people I have given the most to in terms of time, prayer, and concern are the people who end up leaving for unhappy reasons. To some degree I am wary of needy people who begin attending the church and indicate their needs in varies ways. It is almost that I know what is coming and am reluctant to be involved. I do put myself out there and become involved, of course, but I am now ready for surprises and disappointments.

Another possible reason for the anger that comes to pastors is people will take out their rebellion and express aspects of their fallen nature toward the pastor. Pastors may be viewed as an authority figure, even a parental substitute, to which rebellion may be directed. In psychological terms this is called "transference," or, it may be stated like this: people who have unresolved spiritual or psychological issues may unconsciously redirect their conflict toward a pastor. Understanding this process protects me to some degree but not completely, more often I will not understand the spiritual and psychological dynamics being played out around me.

Another source of anger has to do with performance anxiety or the fear of speaking in public. Anxiety can have enormous consequences if not dealt with. It can be a source of anger if not frustration and stress. It is well known that public speaking is one of the high anxiety activities that humans engage in. Although I have been preaching and teaching for 33 years I still become anxious on Sunday morning. Sometimes Saturday night I have a difficult time sleeping. Sometimes that depends on how I feel about the sermon, but any time I have to speak before a group I will have some anxiety.

One Sunday morning, after studying my sermons, I began to pray that God would fill me with His Spirit that I might proclaim the gospel. After the prayer a strong sense of anxiety descended upon me. It had to do with the fact I did not know what I would preach the following Sunday, either morning or evening. That anxiety nearly got to me until I remembered the passage in the Lord's prayer about asking for bread for that day. I would concern myself with the sermons I needed on Monday morning.

I do not experience as much anxiety when I am teaching a Bible study or leading a workshop. The television program brings out some anxiety. Some weddings and funerals are quite stressful and anxiety producing. It is characteristic of me in those circumstances that I will butcher a word or two before I feel confident. Also, I have anxiety before church council meetings, even when there is nothing serious on the agenda. Merely being in front of a group of people produces stress and anxiety, and anger may follow close behind.

Anger may come up suddenly. On more than a few occasions I have been the picture of pastoral tranquility at one moment and flash angry the next. I am aware there is anger in me. This knowledge is to my advantage because it helps me recognize anger when it comes up and thereby I am better able to cope with it. My desire is to follow the admonition of the Scripture and not allow the sun to go down on my anger.

Anxiety and stress can not be avoided certainly. Pastors must preach, teach, lead worship, conduct meetings, and officiate at weddings and funerals. One thing I do is bring my anxiety and anger to Jesus since I know He cares for me; yet, I find that I still have some anxiety. Without the resources that are mine in Christ the anxiety might overwhelm me altogether. I have known pastors whose anxiety level was so high it prevented them from being preachers of the gospel for a period of time. Though I will have some anxiety, be stressed out, and feel anger, I am still able to move ahead. I find it helps to face the reality of these ugly, unpleasant things. The "peace of God that passes understanding" is indeed real. I do have that peace, that peace of knowing my sin is covered and that I have eternal life in Jesus. This is the peace that I have. But mental and emotional tranquility is not always mine. I go on whether I have it or not.

There is yet another type of anger, too, something professionals call "passive-aggressive anger." This occurs in a circumstance where anger ought to be expressed, but for various reasons, it is not.

Pastors learn quickly enough not to express anger to the church. Pastors are thought by some to be super saints, occasionally walking on water, and, never angry. Though Jesus is described as being angry on several different occasions, pastors are not allowed to be angry. If a pastor is overcome with anger in front of members of the congregation, that pastor will pay a heavy price for it. For some, it is never forgotten, and remains inexcusable. I know this from first hand experience.

Pastors therefore repress the anger they feel even under circumstances where an acknowledgment of anger would be healthy. There is a dilemma for pastors as to what to do with their anger: should it be expressed or repressed? Anger denied or repressed will come out in some way, usually in the form of anxiety or depression. It can even lead to addictive behaviors like overeating, alcohol, or drug abuse—even sexual immorality. In general, repressed anger can surface as depression or as an overwhelming experience of discouragement. Anger acted out can result in violence or addictive, destructive behavior.

Many people would be surprised that pastors could have some of these problems. In my volunteer work at San Quentin Prison I have known convicts who had been pastors, genuine born again Christians, but whose anger mastered them. Some committed a violent crime, even murder.

Pastors are human beings and are often unaware of the unconscious processes that go on within them. Some pastors will spiritualize problems thus denying their vulnerability. This is a great mistake.

When trouble comes pastors could benefit from having someone to talk with who might help relieve their stress, anxiety, and anger. Let me restate something from another chapter—a pastor does not want to develop a confessor or confidant within the church. That can go on to a mild degree, but any more would be a mistake. Church members, usually, should not be burdened with the struggles of their pastor. Professionals, people trained to work with people with problems, have trouble with it. Pastors have been terribly disappointed and damaged thinking they were safe with a deacon, an elder, another pastor, or a member of the staff. If a pastor is struggling with depression, discouragement, anger, or anything else, it is best to go outside the church to someone unknown and pay for counsel. Many denominations provide counseling services. If that is so, fine, but if it were me I would probably find someone in another town I did not know and who did not know me; I would go to them for counsel.

I am not negating the power of the cross. We have our fullness in Jesus, and we can always go to Him and lay our anxiety and anger at the foot of His cross. This is the privilege of the child of God. Sometimes, though, it helps to have another human being to talk to as well. The Word of God does encourage the bearing one another's burdens. (Galatians 6:2) All that is needed sometimes is for another person to know, and understand to some degree, the nature of our struggle.

☞ Have you ever seen a pastor angry?

☞ Can you imagine that you would ever be angry?

☞ Are you angry now?

☞ Do you have anyone you can talk to about it?

Forty-seven

# Theological Models

"Brother, I just believe the whole Word of God. Don't you?"

"Sure, but I am not convinced the only inspired version of the Bible is the King James. Look here, I have a KJV on my shelf. It is the very Bible I started preaching with. Is that good enough for you?"

"Well, it is better than the other apostate versions, but your edition doesn't have the Scofield notes. No, I can't attend here. There is not one good church in this whole county. I'll stay home and watch a TV preacher."

✛    ✛    ✛    ✛    ✛

I did not know the difference between a Catholic and a Baptist prior to my conversion; I was, theologically speaking, a blank page. Early on I embraced Arminian views and generally rejected what I thought was Calvinistic or Reformed theology.

My conversion took place in a Southern Baptist Church and during my six years at a Southern Baptist Seminary I adhered to the Arminian viewpoint presented there. As a non-denominational independent during the 1970s, with a newly acquired charismatic/pentecostal orientation, I still felt comfortable with my

Arminian position. During that period I was at various times a dispensational premillenialist, an historical premillenialist, and an amillenialist. Recently I have been examining postmillennial views held by the Puritans of the seventeenth and eighteenth centuries. (I must have been right at some point, I just don't know when.) I have largely shifted from my Arminian views to embrace a more "reformed" theology though I have been referred to as "reforming" as opposed to "reformed"

I have had, then, different theological models through which I view the Scripture and around which I form a systematic theology. It is like putting on a pair of glasses. The model, paradigm, or theological system is the pair of glasses we see the Bible through. Among the "pairs of glasses" that could be put on are: a *Pentecostal* model— everything is seen through an emphasis on the Holy Spirit. There is a *holiness* model; the necessity of personal holiness is the controlling factor. There is the *Arminian* model that emphasizes free will, and there is the *Reformed* model that emphasizes the free grace and sovereignty of God. There are models with a focus on the last days, the *pre-millennial, post-millennial, and amillennial theories.* There are *dispensational and covenant* views. (Indeed, there are many others, e.g., *Process Theology, Liberation Theology,* on the liberal side of things.) I feel that clinging to one in complete rejection of all of the others is not always a safe and sound position, especially for the pastor of a church. Rigid adherence to one system may distort our view of the Bible, and in extreme cases, may result in a cultic mentality. It is not uncommon for pastors who are bound to a particular system to exclude, albeit unintentionally, those who differ on even a minor point. This can be quite dangerous, and will result, finally, in an unhealthy church. I have my views certainly, from which I will not be moved, but an uncritical commitment to a human system is not the same as devotion to Christ.

As a kid my heroes were the Hollywood cowboys, Roy Rogers, Gene Autry, the Cisco Kid, and The Lone Ranger. I have my heroes now, too, George Whitefield, John Wesley, Jonathan Edwards, Samuel Davies—in fact, almost all the great figures of the First Great Awakening in America. Then there is Asahel Nettleton, Timothy Dwight, and Peter Cartwright of the Second Great Awakening in America, among others. David Martyn Lloyd-Jones, a.k.a. "the Doctor" and "the last of the Puritans" has greatly influenced me. Perhaps the person I hold in highest esteem is Charles H. Spurgeon, the "prince of preachers".

Charles H. Spurgeon, pastor of Park Street and the Metropolitan Baptist churches of London, accepted paradoxes; he preached two biblical truths at once that seemed contradictory because the Scripture, he believed, taught both. For instance, the Scripture teaches that people are unable to come to Jesus for salvation on their own. Furthermore, the Scripture teaches that God even supplies the faith to trust in Jesus in that the Holy Spirit of God must convict of sin and reveal the Savior. Yet, every human is asked, commanded even, to trust in Jesus and His shed blood for the forgiveness of sin. Both the hyper-Calvinists and Arminians of Spurgeon's day attacked him. Both camps thought he was not being true to their models. The hyper-Calvinists objected to Spurgeon's urging unconverted people to come to Christ, and the Arminians objected to Spurgeon's refusal to name a concrete way in which the new birth might be obtained. A true Calvinist, he preached that a person must come to Jesus but knew that the Holy Spirit alone could accomplish that. Yet Spurgeon would plead long and eloquently with the unconverted for them to come to Jesus for salvation.

Similarly, I do not want to defend a theological position that forces me to reject straightforward biblical truth. It has seemed to me that not all the points of the major models are blatantly and clearly biblical however internally consistent they might appear. Though the doctrinal points in any system tend to be logical and mutually dependent, I am not necessarily persuaded by logical arguments on points of doctrine. Doctrine must flow easily and plainly from the Scripture. Consistency of logic is not a requirement or test for truth.

There are numerous paradoxes in the Scripture that defy our reason. The paradox concerning Jesus for instance—Jesus is God and man at once. Also, the Bible is the Word of God but written by man—to me this is a paradox. There are paradoxes connected with almost every major point of theology. The paradox surrounding conversion may be the most baffling yet important one of them all.

Let me be clear: my suggestion is to avoid the wholesale adoption of any one theological model.

The problem is that denominations, fellowship groups, associations, and educational institutions will often subscribe to one particular model or another. And often acceptance and fellowship will be built around that. I have a difficult time participating in some Christian fellowship groups because somewhere along the line I will reveal who I am and will thereby run into trouble, most often rejection. If someone thinks that I am a thoroughgoing Arminian they will find me embracing Reformed views. If I am with a group of ministers who are given to a hyper-Calvinistic doctrine they may find what they consider to be Arminianism in me. Of course, fellowship is at risk. Consequently I look for fellowship with groups that are inclusive. Some groups are openly *anti-Pentecostal or anti-Charismatic* and I am uncomfortable with that. Some groups think little of those who, in their opinion, are not actively practicing the gifts of the Spirit. Additionally, I am uncomfortable with situations where conversation has to be coached in a particular kind of language, that is, insisting, perhaps unconsciously, on the use of insider language and buzzwords.

It may be that I do not fit in any place. There is not one model that reflects all that I see in Scripture. And so I am careful at this stage of my ministry not to identify myself so very completely with any one theological model.

At Miller Avenue there are any number of different theological models represented in the congregation. Some have a fairly fixed model; others do not and do not care that they don't. It is not my goal to have everyone conform to the exact pattern of belief that I have. Yes, the Apostle's Creed is our standard and the Bible is our final authority for faith and practice. But I do not want to force people into anything. My experience has been that as the Word of God is preached and taught the hearers will be instructed by the Holy Spirit and adopt biblical doctrines as their own. I can not become anxious about this process. People must be free to express their views without fear of censor, criticism, or rejection.

Jesus must be the center and focus of fellowship; I am more interested in what a person thinks of Jesus than anything else. If a person loves Jesus and is resting and trusting in His free grace, I have found that I can live with their theological model though it might differ from my own.

☞ Do you have a theological model?

☞ Are you comfortable with it?

☞ Would you run into trouble if you varied from it?

Forty-eight

# Church Discipline

"Kent, I hear there is sin being practiced at your church." One of my colleagues announced at the monthly ministerial meeting.

"I wouldn't be surprised." I returned. "How do you know?"

"That's confidential. What are your going to do about it?"

"Not that there isn't some sin at the church, but I am not aware of anything in particular. Maybe you could help me?"

"No, no. That's not my job. But you'd better get busy and find out about it because it involves one of your pastors. I think there will be a lot of repenting to do."

My association with pastors of many different denominations over more than thirty years demonstrates that approaches to church discipline vary greatly. My approach has varied also.

A Matthew 18 approach to church discipline is rare. In that passage, Jesus outlined a process whereby wrongs are to be made right. First, the parties in conflict are to work out the problem between them. Failing at this initial stage, a few others are to enter the process. Lastly, if the issue is yet unresolved the entire church is to be brought in.

Matthew 18 applies specifically, I believe, to a local church situation. (However, it may be practiced in any personal situation outside the church as well. It is a sound approach to conflict resolution in any venue.) It does not necessarily apply, I believe, beyond that. For example, I am not required biblically to follow the Matthew 18 process with Sun Young Moon of the Unification Church. His false doctrine is published before the whole world not to me alone. I am then free to counter him publicly without resort to Matthew 18.

If a problem comes to the attention of a pastor, that is, two people are willing to submit an issue to a pastor, generally a resolution can be reached and that is the end of it. In my experience that have been only a few occasions when a conflict had to be brought before the congregation.

There was a time at Miller Avenue when a conflict remained unresolved and thus moved on to the church council. This particular situation resulted in fourteen people leaving the church. A prominent member claimed to have had a vision in which he saw himself as the "Rock of Miller Avenue." He succeeded in getting a dozen people to believe him. Naturally, I would have had to resign as pastor; but I refused, of course, to leave. The situation was painfully resolved; I remained and the "rock" left. But it came down to one vote. The "chemistry" of the church suffered for many years after as a result.

There are churches, which have no formal church disciplinary process in place or if they do, they are reluctant to follow it. This is not unusual at all; in fact, this is the way most churches operate. Any "discipline" that takes place in such a church is accidental and/or unintentional. And, at the risk of seeming unbiblical and liberal, let me say that such an approach is not altogether without merit.

Problems will be resolved one way or another and often the simple process of time will take care of many of them. This process has worked well for me dozens of times particularly when the principles were fairly familiar with the scriptural teaching on church discipline. My approach of standing back and not interfering has worked. If I get involved I have noticed that things tend to escalate. I will remain on the sidelines unless or until I am directly requested to enter the process. However, in my early years I would routinely get involved in other people's squabbles even to the point of demanding that issues be laid before the "elders." Despite consistently poor, even disastrous, results, I persisted in the practice until a wise seminary professor showed me the error of my ways.

My preference is to slow and easy going. Once a church is committed to censoring people, correcting them and finally excommunicating them, a great deal of time and energy will be spent in church discipline. It quickly becomes a Pandora's Box. "Head hunting" is a phrase that comes to mind and when a church starts down that road more than a few heads will be found that need to be loped off.

Crazy things may go on in churches because unconverted people and converted people who are struggling with their fallen nature are mixed in with, hopefully, a few mature Christians. If a church and/or pastor starts looking for sin in the church it will not be hard to find. And then what do you do?

The Holy Spirit does what no human can do. I can pound on the pulpit, pull my hair, interfere and complain, even threaten, but the Holy Spirit, when there is sound Bible teaching and preaching, has a way of making corrections in people's lives.

A genuine problem, however, and one that can not be avoided, is open sin being practiced and promoted by someone in the church. At the Corinthian church, for example, a man lived with his father's wife—a stepmother. The sin, known to all in the church, was at some level accepted; some were even bragging or boasting about their "maturity" in being able to tolerate the behavior. For Paul this was going too far, so he urged church discipline.

As a pastor I know the sins of the people in the congregation all too well. Not that people are divulging or confessing them, but the areas of vulnerability and weakness are usually fairly clear for an experienced sinner like me to spot. What sins have not I myself been guilty of or tempted by or somehow familiar with? But if a blatant rebellion is going on, and it is being accepted—a particular sin is even being promoted—then steps must be taken or the church will suffer.

Christians are capable of the most egregious sins. Because someone had a terrible moral breakdown I do not assume the person is not a genuinely converted person. Only time will tell and that time may not come around until the judgment. Peter was guilty of a great sin—actual betrayal of Jesus. Yet, he repented. The person living with his stepmother was eventually excommunicated, he repented, and Paul had to ask the Corinthian Church to readmit him into fellowship. Neither initially nor subsequently are we saved by works. Pastors must be aware that people in the church will sin and the real issue is—what then? The overriding interest must be restoration.

False doctrine must also be countered and quickly. Miller Avenue holds to the commonly accepted Apostle's Creed, which gives us a means of evaluating doctrine. In fact, the Apostle's Creed appears on two banners that are at the front of the building. If someone advocated a doctrine that deviated from the Apostle's Creed, or placed undo emphasis on a particular doctrine, I would first talk to the individual and try to reach some point of agreement. If that proved futile, I would invite two or three other people to join with me in the process. If that also failed, I would take the matter to the church council. If no resolution emerged, the person would be asked to withdraw from the church. This is an extreme situation; I have had to do it a couple of times and regardless of how carefully things are done, it turns out to be an unpleasant experience.

In the case of "The Rock of Miller Avenue," what if he had not left the church on his own. Suppose he had continued to attend services and continually sought to win others to his position. Though I have never been faced with such a predicament, it seems clear the entire congregation would have to be exposed to the issue. Then, of course, there is a risk of losing more people. In addition, blocks of time would be spent in meetings, phone conversations, and so on. Some people are very offended when something goes wrong in a church; they make some strange thing out of it. They might wonder, "Where is the love of Jesus here?"

This is my suggestion: Inform the person he/she is trespassing and that a warning has been issued. If the warning is not heeded, I would, in fact, right there on Sunday morning, call the police and have the person removed from the premises. This would be, of course, with the knowledge, backing and approval of the church council. In only one case did I have to resort to such a threat and thankfully it was sufficient. Such an extreme measure is dreadful in itself, but the pastor has a responsibility to protect the church.

One of my errors has been not taking time to get to know new people and not giving appropriate time for new people to get to know the church before inviting them into some ministry responsibility. I am commonly overly impressed by appearances. Some time has to expire now, time to see if the person is either the genuine article or something else. Before a person is invited to preach, teach, or lead a group, a considerable amount of time must elapse before I open up ministry opportunities. For example, people are often attracted to the San Quentin ministry. My response is, "Keep attending for a few months, let us get to know you, and you get to know us, and we will talk about any possible involvement at the prison."

This simple essay on church discipline is far from the best and last word on the subject, and frankly, my experience is more limited than the first paragraph of this chapter might imply. The Scripture teaches me to go to Matthew 18, often though, I follow the "do little or do nothing" philosophy. The latter approach generally will work well enough so that the full Matthew 18 process can be saved for extreme cases.

✤　✤　✤　✤　✤

☞ Can you describe an instance of church discipline you personally witnessed?

☞ How did it work out?

☞ How would you minister to a member of the church who was actively engaged in blatant sin?

☞ How about a staff member?

☞ How about a member of your own family?

☞ How would you like to be dealt with if you had a problem?

Forty-nine

# On Being Politically Correct

"Will you include this prayer to the earth goddess Gaia in our wedding ceremony Kent?" the bride asked.

"Gaia, who is Gaia?" I wanted to know.

"The earth goddess, the feminine deity. We are spiritual people, not religious of course, but very spiritual and we want this in our ceremony."

"I wish I could, but this is not the God of the Bible. The earth is part of His creation. I can and will do a lot of things, but I can not go this far. Perhaps I can recommend someone who would be willing to do it."

✛　　✛　　✛　　✛　　✛

Should the gospel preacher be politically correct? Yes! Did my answer surprise you?

There is little hope I am politically correct at all times, but I want to be when and where it will honor and glorify God.

The gospel message has enough offense built into it. The biblical emphasis on repentance, the necessity to turn from sin, is objectionable to the unconverted. That Jesus, very God and Man at once, is the only way of salvation is a major stumbling block to millions of people.

I remember how offended I was at the preaching of Bob Lewis, my first pastor, while in my unconverted state. It was almost more than I could take at times. The gospel preacher does not need to exacerbate the situation by adding points extraneous to the gospel that are politically or socially sensitive.

There are limits to how politically correct I will be, of course. I will not embrace the move for inclusive language (nonsexist and non-gender terms) in Scripture and hymns. Nor will I minimize that there is salvation in Jesus alone. I will not reduce Miller Avenue to a recovery center or entertainment mecca; Miller Avenue will not become another kiosk in the booming spiritual shopping mall. However, I am appalled when I hear unkind, even inflammatory words in sermons being spoken that are absolutely unnecessary. Attacks against individuals, denominations, and churches in public meetings are rarely if ever helpful, but are more likely to build walls that prevent people from hearing the real message of the gospel. (I will name cults and cult leaders readily enough since one of my jobs is to protect the sheep.) Labels referencing gender, ethnic origin, socioeconomic or educational levels, and other stereotypical allusions, even if intended to be humorous, close hearts and minds to the gospel.

I am aware that political correctness is often considered to be little more than a social/political fad championed by "liberals". It seems that the preacher of the gospel will be mindful, however, that all have sinned and fall short of the glory of God, and that our God is longsuffering towards all sinners. And it is His will that none should perish but that all would come to repentance. Our God is compassionate and graciously receives all who come to Him. Our God causes the heavens to rejoice when one lost person is found. This is the nature of our God, and the preacher of the gospel will not want to put any artificial barriers in the way of anyone when presenting the gospel. The gospel is offense enough.

Let me call attention to two passages in 1 Corinthians, which support this point. In 1 Corinthians 9:19-22 Paul writes:

> Though I am free and belong to no man, I make myself a slave to everyone, to win as many as possible. To the Jews I became like a Jew, to win the Jews. To those under the law I became like one under the law (though I myself am not under the law), so as to win those under the law. To those not having the law I became like one not having the law (though I am not free from God's law but am under Christ's law), so as to win those not having the law. To the weak I became weak, to win the weak. I have become all things to all men so that by all possible means I might save some.

A second passage is 1 Corinthians 10:31-32.

> So whether you eat or drink or whatever you do, do it all for the glory of God. Do not cause anyone to stumble, whether Jews, Greeks, or the Church of God—even as I try to please everybody in every way. For I am not seeking my own good but the good of many, so that they may be saved.

Paul loved to preach the gospel, that gospel which had so offended him while he was Saul. Now, however, he would build no barriers so that everyone might be saved.

Gospel preachers may follow Paul's example and avoid artificial offenses that really do not belong to the gospel so that people will hear the voice of Jesus and hopefully be converted.

☞ How does the phrase, "politically correct" strike you?

☞ How politically correct do you think you are? Do you care?

# Fifty

# Avoiding Magical Thinking

"If America is going to be saved, we all have to humble ourselves before God. If we do this, our land will be healed. Kent, will you be on our committee to get this done?"

"What would you like me to do?"

"We need you to get your church on board and then visit other pastors and get them committed. If we get all the churches, or most of them anyway, praying for renewal— then God must bless us. Don't you believe that?"

"No!"

✠     ✠     ✠     ✠     ✠

Earlier I referred to conversion as a mystery. We do not deal well with mysteries—we like to solve them. We do not do well with paradoxes either, we like to simplify, and we have been particularly guilty of this when it comes to conversion. A result of the damage caused by ignoring the mysterious and paradoxical nature of conversion is what I call "magical thinking."

It is my concern that the people to whom I preach would never hear Jesus say, "I never knew you. Away from me, you evildoers." (see Matthew 7:23) I would prefer they would hear Jesus say, "Well done, good and faithful servant. Come and share your master's happiness!" (see Matthew 25:21) That is the primary responsibility of the pastoral ministry. It is of no value to shepherd people through life who are unconverted. It is not my job to make people feel comfortable and at ease. My task is to present the gospel so that people are converted.

Consequently it is essential to avoid "magical thinking" about conversion. We cannot think that simply uttering a prayer, even the popular "sinner's prayer" will automatically result in conversion. This is not to say it will not, however. I prayed a version of the "sinner's prayer" and was not converted for nine months; my father, however, prayed the "sinner's prayer" at a Billy Graham Crusade and was converted on the spot. Over the course of three decades I have prayed with many people, hundreds of people, and all were not necessarily much less automatically converted. At least this became evident over a period of time that such was the case when there was no life of the Holy Spirit in the individual. No love for the Scripture, no love for prayer, no love for Jesus, no love for worship; these were absent in many I had prayed with. It is not a stretch of the imagination to assume that no conversion took place.

But the dominant evangelical thinking many of us inherited is that conversion must result when a person has "accepted" Jesus. If a person has good theology, whether it is Arminian or Reformed, attests to an historical creed and lives and acts like a Christian— this "work" must surely indicate true conversion. This is what I refer to as magical thinking. Being a baptized, communicant church member and doing good works does not mean conversion is in place. Salvation is by grace, God's own work. Human effort can not guarantee conversion. God is not obligated to give eternal life on the basis of any work however sincere and devoted.

Conversion is something that God brings and it has nothing to do with our work. Remember Ephesians 2:8-9, "For it is by grace you have been saved, through faith—and this not from yourselves, it is the gift of God--not by works, so that no one can boast." Grace we know is God given, a gift, and faith must be too or grace would no longer be grace. Certainly, it is magical thinking that says a person can earn salvation.

Magical thinking must be avoided in regards to revival, too. John Armstrong, in *When God Moves*, published by Harvest House, brings this truth very forcibly. He states, "Revival is not guaranteed though the whole nation would repent." Nothing can guarantee revival. There are no methods, measures, or works that guarantee revival. Revival is something that God brings supernaturally, and sovereignly. We cannot manipulate God.

There are revival times and there are "normal" times. In normal times few are converted. In normal times years may fly by and the strongest gospel preaching and most diligent efforts may bring little or no result. In revival times, though, many are converted. In the great awakenings, or revivals, in America, thousands were converted in short periods of time. Revival is going on somewhere in the world nearly all the time; these are special and unusual moves of God.

It is helpful to remember the lessons Scripture and history teach. However hard I might preach, however holy a life I may live, however prayerful and steadfast the church may be—these guarantee neither conversions nor revival. Yet, these are to be continually sought after and practiced.

Whether we minister in normal or revival times we are called to be faithful in preaching the Gospel, pastoring the congregation, and leading the church in praise, worship, and service.

☞ What do you think of the notion, "magical thinking?"

☞ Is the term misapplied?

☞ What word or phrase might serve as a synonym?

☞ Does the distinction between normal and revival times seem justified?

Fifty-one

# A Sermon to Have Ready to Preach

Both young men, tattooed on arms, legs, back, chest, and neck, looked at me in stunned silence. "A sermon, you're going to preach a sermon?"

"If you want me to."

"I've heard all the sermons I want to hear, man, and you don't look like any preacher."

"Let him preach the sermon," came a voice from the next cell. "What do you have to lose. You got no TV in there anyway."

✥     ✥     ✥     ✥     ✥

Preachers of the gospel need at least one good sermon ready for any occasion. This chapter consists of a paraphrase of one I use. The occasion could be a church worship service, but it could be a small group or even a single individual. Though the sermon is directed to the unconverted, believers also benefit from hearing a clear gospel message.

The original sermon is titled "*The Theology of New Birth*," by Jonathan Dickinson. He was pastor of the Presbyterian Church of Elizabethtown, New Jersey. In 1741, at the height of the First Great Awakening in America, Dickinson preached this sermon. One of the leading Puritan preachers, he served as the first president of Princeton University. In the sermon he described the view of conversion, as it was understood by the "moderate" Calvinists of his day.

My paraphrases are different each time. This paraphrase differs from the one in my earlier book, *Are You Really Born Again?* I have a two or three minute version, a five-minute version, a ten-minute version, and then I have a version that can last over an hour. The sermon lends itself to versatility and is another reason it is so useful.

I am a volunteer with "Prison Bible Studies" at San Quentin Prison. Several of us at Miller Avenue have been a part of this ministry for over a decade. We are assigned cellblocks within the prison and are able to walk the tiers and talk to the inmates. My method is to walk down a tier without looking into the cells. I am waiting for someone to invite me over and in a very short time a call will come. After introductions and some casual conversation (there are always two people in a cell, at least that is the way it has been for years now due to overcrowding), I will say to them, "Would you like to hear a sermon?" And I have never, ever, not one time, been told, "No we do not want to hear the sermon!" And I ask both men; they both have to agree they want to hear the sermon.

Before the delivery of the sermon I give instructions. "There are five points, and I am going to ask you to remember all five plus the name of the man who wrote the sermon, the name of the sermon, and the year in which it was preached." Afterwards I will go back over the points with them. The inmates will then get the ten-minute version and that is the one presented here.

## The Theology of New Birth
## By Jonathan Dickinson, 1741
## A Paraphrase by Kent Philpott

The text for the sermon is 1 Peter 1:23, "For you have been born again, not of perishable seed, but of imperishable, through the living and enduring word of God."

The first point is: *you must realize your own miserable condition and see it as it is.* It is the Holy Spirit who convicts of sin, shows us we have sinned against a holy and righteous God. We see that our sin has offended the God who loves us. We have committed a crime against God. Our breaking of God's law has resulted in condemnation; we have been arrested, tried, judged, and incarcerated on condemned row, and there is no human possibility of the sentence ever being reversed. There is no escape, either.

It takes the Holy Spirit to show us this because we never come to such a conclusion on our own. At best we are remorseful. We may feel sorry—sorry particularly that we got caught, unhappy that we find ourselves in a depressing and discouraging circumstance. But it is the Holy Spirit who will show us our sin in such a way that we can truly repent. Repentance acknowledges that we have offended God. This is the truth about our situation and no one, no judge, no lawyer, no amount of money can change one detail. This is the first point.

Point two is: *you now see your situation is hopeless.* There is no appeal, no defense, no hope whatsoever. Finished! Absolutely hopeless! No writ can be filed with any court that will take us off the row.

We realize that all attempts at being righteous are completely futile. The only course is surrender; all

232

efforts for securing righteousness come to an end. Even religious devotion, more Bible reading, more church, more prayer, more good works, is now abandoned; any pretense of goodness is given up. There is no more thought of "turning over a new leaf."

All bargaining is rejected as hopeless; the only prospect is judgment and rejection by God. This is the second point.

The third point is: *you now have an "interest in Jesus."* The puritans would refer to a person at this point as being in a "pre-awakened" state. Prior to this, Jesus was thought of as "a great teacher," "founder of a religion," "a great prophet," He even may have been referred to as "the Messiah," but now we see, by the illumination of the Holy Spirit, who Jesus actually is. Due to the darkened understanding brought about by the fallen nature and sin, we always do some strange thing with Jesus. But the Spirit of God reveals that Jesus is the only hope, that Jesus is, in fact, *the Savior.* The truth of the gospel is now experienced in a most personal way. Jesus is seen as the one whose shed blood is powerful to cleanse from sin and remove it permanently. Jesus' work of dying as our substitute, being buried, and rising from the dead and now being at the right hand of the Father in heaven is impressed upon us. Jesus, the living Savior, has the power and authority to save right now!

This biblical view of Jesus can only be made clear to the heart and mind through the Holy Spirit! We will not come to it apart from Him. Remember that the Scripture declares "we are dead in our trespasses and sins." Therefore, it is the Holy Spirit who draws us to Jesus. Jesus said, "No one can come to me unless the Father who sent me draws him." When the Holy Spirit reveals Jesus to us, when we see our hopelessness, then by His power we are able to come to Jesus. This is the third point.

The fourth point is: y*ou must come to Jesus and be converted.* Salvation does belong solely to God! It is only by His leading, by His inspiration, by His revelation of our sin and of Jesus as the Savior that conversion occurs. There is a great mystery to conversion, but we know we can not accomplish it ourselves any more than we could cause ourselves to be physically born.

Dickinson did not say, "If you will pray this prayer, you will be converted" or "If you will join the church you will be forgiven" or "If you are baptized you will be forgiven" or "If you _____, then you will have eternal life." Dickinson would make none of those statements, and the great Puritan preachers in the awakenings would make none of those statements. The Awakening preachers presented the gospel and depended upon God's Holy Spirit to bring conversion. So often false conversions arise when anything less occurs. And so you must come to Jesus. You must repent of your sin and trust in Jesus. I will not ask either of you to pray with me except that God's Spirit will show you your sin and reveal Jesus to you. Your conversion must rest solely upon Jesus and His shed blood and not on any work of your own. I can not bring you pardon or salvation. You must be born again of the Spirit of God. Just as you had nothing to do with your own birth, likewise you cannot do anything to bring about the new birth. Are you born again, have you ever come to Jesus for forgiveness? If not, you can pray right now that the Holy Spirit will cause you to be born again, help you repent and trust is Jesus as Savior. This is the fourth point.

The fifth point is: *sanctification.* Sanctification is "attaining to the whole measure of the fullness of

Christ." This is a lifelong process. At the moment of conversion we are declared righteous. We are "placed in Jesus;" His righteousness is *imputed* to us—given to us. This is what it means to be "justified." We still have no righteousness of our own. All of our righteousness is in Jesus. We begin by faith and we live our lives by faith, meaning we trust and abide in Jesus. He is our sanctification. We become His disciples. We read the Scripture and follow His commands, we seek to be obedient to the word of God, and God works in us so that we will grow up into Jesus. We remain sinners and sinless at the same time. All of my sin has been washed away in the blood of Jesus— past, present, and future; yet we are told to confess our sins in 1 John 1:9. We are to confess our sins and turn away from our sins, keeping our consciences clear. There is a paradox—we are perfect yet sinners all at the same time. But we rest and abide in the *finished work of Jesus,* not trusting the flesh. The flesh will fail us. We have a fallen nature, and it will rise up and trouble us from time to time, and Satan will accuse us of being hypocrites pointing out our failures to live the Christian life. Sometimes I have thought, "I should not go down to that church and be with those good people. I am too great a sinner to be associated with those good people who live those good lives." We reject the attacks of Satan and especially those condemnations from our own minds and continue to trust and follow Jesus even after we have experienced a terrible defeat.

We will grow up into the fullness of Jesus because it is the will of our Father in heaven. We have the sanctification God's Holy Spirit works into our lives daily, a little bit at a time. This is the fifth point.

This is a sermon to have ready to preach.

✛   ✛   ✛   ✛   ✛

☞ How might a converted person benefit from hearing this sermon?

☞ Is this a sermon you might preach?

☞ How might you alter it?

Fifty-two

# The Pastor as A Suffering Servant*

"If it's that bad, why don't you quit the church?"

I wished I had shut up. I never should have exposed myself to the degree I did. He seemed so sympathetic at first. I hope he doesn't start talking to other people about me. And it all started when I did a little whining in the sermon last Sunday. When will I learn?

✠ ✠ ✠ ✠ ✠

Jesus, according to the prophet Isaiah, chapter 53, is the suffering servant of Israel, a man of sorrows who would take the sin of the people upon Himself. Jesus, the great shepherd of the sheep, leaves His under-shepherds a great example. No one has suffered or will suffer like Jesus when He poured out His life to death and experienced the "wages" of our sin. To suffering, though not nearly to the degree experienced by Jesus, every pastor is called.

Perhaps the most important sermon pastors preach is the living out of their own lives. A pastor lives a public life, in full view of both church and community. Many will witness the triumphs and defeats and will, in some fashion, identify with and learn from these. A pastor will become a "spectacle" often spoken for or against

237

and, at very least, will be a topic of communal conversation. Both the converted and the unconverted will want to see if Jesus meets the real life needs of the pastor. Thus the pastor can not, must not, live an aloof, private, and hidden life.

Pastors have become frustrated, angry, and even given up, when it became clear that living such an "infamous" public life was unavoidable.

A pastor's life and struggles should not, however, be a "centerpiece" of community and congregational attention. I mean, the pastor's life experiences should not frequently form the skeleton around which sermons, or sermon illustrations, are built. (Many would argue the reverse.) Such a practice, if it became something of an ongoing saga, might result in a kind of spiritual narcissism that would detract from a gospel witness.

Church members may learn how to deal with their own sufferings and trials by observing how pastors deal with their own. Paul taught that God would comfort people in their sufferings so that others might be comforted. (see 2 Corinthians 1:4) In verse 6 we find: "If we are distressed, it is for your comfort and salvation; if we are comforted, it is for your comfort, which produces in you patient endurance of the same sufferings we suffer."

What trouble will a pastor experience? There is the built-in offense of the gospel that the unconverted, and rebellious Christians unhappily, will direct toward the preacher of that gospel. When the message is despised the easiest out for the offended is to attack the messenger. All preachers figure this out in due time but it hurts nevertheless. Then there is the working out of "growing pains" that young and immature Christians normally experience. Of course, the pastor as spiritual authority will bear the brunt of this. If I were to develop this point it could run into the dozens of pages. Also, there is the pastor's personal experience of growing up into Jesus, particularly the continual confrontation with sinfulness and pride. Additionally, there is the process of life itself—aging, disease, various traumas, and finally dying.

Spurgeon, bed ridden for most of the last years of his short life, discretely shared his pain and suffering in some sermons. He never looked for pity; rather he constantly praised God who was his strength. Indeed, God's power was evident in Spurgeon's weakness much the way it was for the Apostle Paul.

Church members will read of Jesus, Paul, and other great biblical characters, they will read the biographies of renowned saints, but they will observe their pastor. How the pastor follows Jesus in good times and bad will be the loudest, the longest, and the best of sermons.

✥   ✥   ✥   ✥   ✥

☞ What about "suffering in silence"?

☞ Is silence the best policy or can certain experiences be shared with a congregation?

☞ Can you imagine areas to avoid and means of communication that are questionable?

---

*I owe the inspiration for this chapter to Dr. Scott Hafemann, Professor of New Testament at Wheaton College.

Fifty-three

# The Parsonage

"Who is that out there?" I asked my wife. "Oh, I see, never mind. It's some ladies from the church."

"What are they doing out there peeking in the window like that, Kent?"

"I wish I knew. But the big question is how are we going to get them to stop trying to see what goes on in here."

✤　✤　✤　✤　✤

This chapter is for pastors who are fortunate enough to be able to live in a church owned parsonage. "Parsonage is the term American Baptists use. Others may have different terms for the same thing. Manse and rectory, for example, are used. A parsonage is a great benefit for the small church. If Miller Avenue had not built one many years ago, I doubt whether the church would have survived here in this pricey area. But parsonages are becoming a thing of the past. More often now churches help their pastors with a rental or mortgage allowance.

I said "fortunate" in the above paragraph but that may not always describe the situation.

Too many people know I live directly behind the church building, and many find their way to my front door. Sometimes it seems there is no privacy at all, and in the newspapers we read of pastors who are robbed by crooks looking for the offering. More commonly, though, people hoping to be given food, money, or lodging will show up at any time of the day or night.

A misconception floats around our town that Miller Avenue has unlimited resources and all we have to do is scrape some more gold off one of the chandeliers. Then, as I alluded to in the opening vignette, people in the church may be curious about what does on at their parsonage.

Yes, the parsonage does not belong to me. I pay no rent, up-front anyway; the rental value of the house though is figured into my salary. And, I pay social security tax on the rental value of the parsonage.

Some churches allow pastors to rent out the parsonage and use the money to build equity in a home. I would do this if it was possible, but I am reluctant to enter into complex financial agreements with the church. I have seen other pastors do this and it has sometimes been disastrous. My goal is to preach the gospel and so having food, clothing, shelter, and a lot more, I am content.

I do not own a home, and I may not ever be able to. When I leave Miller Avenue I will probably rent or move to an area where I could afford to buy a modest home. (The property values in Mill Valley in particular and Marin County in general are very high.)

For the most part I spend my own money on fixing up and maintaining the parsonage. I would sound like a squeaky wheel if I went to the church council with every little thing. As best I can I keep the place presentable. I have laid some brick, built a grape arbor, put up a fence or two, planted a lawn, taken out some trees, planted other trees, laid out a garden, and worked to prevent the wild winter creek from taking the parsonage's yard downstream. One of the few times I asked the church for help had to do with the creek problem.

And the parsonage does belong to all of us. My family and I live in it, but it is OURS. Without exception, the people at Miller Avenue respect the Philpott's privacy and we are pleased, proud, and thankful to live in the parsonage.

☞ Does a "parsonage" seem like an advantage or disadvantage to you?

☞ If you live in a parsonage, how can you help the congregation know it belongs to them yet preserve your privacy at the same time?

## Fifty-four

# Pride: An Enemy of our Ministry

"Pastor, Stan should preach a sermon on a Sunday morning. He is a very good Bible teacher and we need to have his input.

"Kent, we simply can not see you heading up this program. If your ministry were more successful, well, that would be different. You know the old saying, 'Success breeds success.'"

"We need more energy here, new ideas, a real go-getter type. Now I'm not saying we don't appreciate you pastor, but someone younger, someone who can identify with young people—might help our church grow."

"I heard many of the local pastors are going on a trip to Israel. How come you aren't going pastor?"

"Excuse me, we were looking for the pastor. You must be the janitor, but maybe we could at least leave a message with you?"

"If only everyone could be like you pastor, a really faithful and godly person."

"Kent, that was the best sermon ever. No one can preach like you."

"We would like to visit Miller Avenue. We heard it is a great church."

✢   ✢   ✢   ✢   ✢

There is a common thread running through each of the above. Do you know what it is? If you guessed "pride" you are right.

Having pride is healthy if we mean by it confidence, ego strength, and a sense of well being. Sometimes this is referred to as self-esteem. But this is not what I mean here. The kind of pride under discussion is an exaggerated and mistaken sense of who we are. It is a failure to see ourselves the way God sees us.

An exaggerated pride is an enemy of our ministry. When there is pride in the pastor, there will be pride in the church. Pride is a sermon that is preached. And, over time, the prideful pastor will build a hellish church.

It is neither helpful nor healthy for me to despise or demean my abilities or myself as a person. For instance, I believe my preaching and teaching skills are fair, maybe good. Though not a great pastor, I am probably doing fine. I like to think I am above average in many ways and improving by the grace of God. However, my self-esteem, my sense of personal worth, is to be rooted and grounded in Jesus and the abundant love He has poured into my life. He alone is my strength. If my self-esteem is dependent on my skills and accomplishments, and other's response to them, pride will grow and perhaps come to characterize my life and ministry.

As John Newton wrote in the well-known hymn *Amazing Grace*, I know I am a "worm," and at the same time I am made in the image of God, wonderfully made at that, and I am a child of the King even an ambassador for Christ. I have also been raised up with Christ and seated with Him in the heavenly realms.

Yet, this is all through grace, it is all a gift. And this fact cuts out any ground for boasting on my part. In truth, I deserve God's wrath and condemnation because I have broken His holy law. In Jesus, however, I am what I am. Thanks be to God. And I know that if there be any good thing in me, anything that God is pleased with, the Holy Spirit has worked it into me. My glory is all the cross.

Unhealthy or sinful pride will cause us to be unloving toward others. It will cause us to fear, despise, or reject those who offend us. In fact, pride will result in our being easily offended. It will drive us to seek out applause and recognition. It will love flattery and approval. It will make us feel sorry for ourselves. It will lead us into discouragement, even depression. It will cause us to rejoice in false things rather than in God and our salvation. It will result in others turning from us when they see the ugly expressions of pride in our life.

We are to count others as better than ourselves. We are to take on the gentleness and meekness of Jesus. We are servants and slaves of Christ and his Body, the Church. So then, where is there a place for pride?

A story about John Bunyan, the great English Baptist and author of *Pilgrims Progress*, illustrates the problem of pride for pastors. After Bunyan had finished a sermon and had just descended the pulpit steps, a member of the congregation said to him, "That was a wonderful sermon pastor." Bunyan replied, "I know, the devil told me so before I reached the bottom step." And it seems I have heard the same from time to time. I have also heard, "That was awful, you ought to quit this preaching." Both statements, whether they came from the devil or not have to do with pride. If the sermon was good, well, praise God. If the sermon was not good, well, praise God and strive to preach better.

Sinful pride will make whiners and quitters out of pastors. Sinful pride will artificially build pastors up so they will not realize that their strength comes from the Lord. Hungering for human praise and recognition will leave pastors starving, empty, and finally desperate.

Jesus told His disciples to follow Him, and Paul said we are to grow up into the stature of the fullness of Christ. In light of these great truths, let me ask this question. When you read the gospel accounts of Jesus' life and ministry, do you see pride in Him? When He talked with and taught His disciples and friends, when He reached out to the poor, blind, and lame, when He confronted His religious opponents, when He stood before those seeking His death, do you see pride in Jesus? I think not.

Let us follow Jesus.

✢     ✢     ✢     ✢     ✢

Pride is sneaky, and pride is hard to define. We detect pride in others readily enough, but rarely see it in ourselves.

 How does unholy pride manifest itself in your life?

Fifty-five

# The Filing System

"We need a nursing home for my father. He will need special care, too. Do you have any ideas?"

I didn't have any ideas, but I had plenty of information in a file. "Can you drop by for a few minutes sometime? I'll get my file out and we will see what resources are available."

He did stop by and the old filing system did not fail me.

✢ ✢ ✢ ✢ ✢

At a ministerial meeting many years ago a retired pastor talked about his filing system. Inwardly I scoffed and thought that I would never need such a thing. It seemed to me a waste of time and emphasis. But I was wrong and I wish I had paid more attention to that wise old preacher.

Of course, I have paper or hard files and electronic files, and I find both are helpful. If necessary I can email a file anywhere in the world or I can open a file in my metal cabinet and locate an address for someone who has called me on the phone. By-in-large my hard and electronic files are not duplicates—some information lends itself to storage in my computer and other material is best on paper.

Most of my sermons are filed according to topic. If I had it to do over I would break the topics down more finely; under "general" there are about one hundred sermons, too many really. Though I do not like to re-preach sermons, sometimes I will or I may want to see what I have preached on a subject or passage previously. And I like to see how my theology has changed (matured?) over the years. This is my most important file.

My second most important file is for subjects in general. Here are files on 12 Step programs, therapists, lawyers, accountants, insurance, taxes, doctors, hospitals, nursing facilities, retirement communities, dentists, resources for the homeless, and so on. I consult this file nearly every single day.

There is a file drawer devoted to the business of the church— financial reports, the weekly bulletin, the monthly newsletter, church council and congregational meeting minutes. I have every bulletin as well as every report, newsletter, and financial statement ever issued at Miller Avenue. After my day is over here, it may all be thrown out but the information is available if it is ever needed—and you just never know.

One of the most useful files is the one on cults and over the years I have gathered material on many dozens of them. Certainly most of this material is available over the internet, but there are some groups in my hard file that few are acquainted with.

My correspondence is filed alphabetically. It is rare that I go to this file, but I have a time or two. I do not make memos of my phone conversations, some do, but if I did, the correspondence file might be a suitable depository for them.

Some pastors have maintained a separate file on each member. I do not and I am not sure why except that it seems like a lot of work. Plus, I would not want such a file read by anyone else, and I doubt I would want it to be generally known that I kept a file on everyone. It might seem a little Brave New Worldly.

The impression might be that I could lay my hand on about anything I need. No, but I might be able to if I had a method of cross-referencing my material. Probably it is too late for me now. I would have to take a sabbatical to get the job done, but I would recommend cross-referencing for anyone starting out.

I am most satisfied with my filing system when I am able to come up with the right resource in a time of need. Certainly I can't be personally aware of all that is available in the community, but I can have the information in my file. Perhaps a comprehensive and workable filing system is as close as I get to the notion of professionalism.

☞ If you have a filing system, is it adequate, will it allow you to grow and expand?

☞ How might you develop a cross-reference system?

## Fifty-six

# Refuse to Be Intimidated

"If you keep preaching like you are you will drive people away. The "S" word is especially offensive. Couldn't you use the word 'mistake' or 'error' or something else? 'Disease' is what a lot of people use instead of sin today. Maybe if you keep it positive more people would come to church."

✣　　✣　　✣　　✣　　✣

The person I quoted above had every good intention. He wanted to see the church grow and he thought that if I used a more "positive" approach people would come into the church.

It is true that there is a tendency among many to substitute "disease" for sin. In Alcoholics Anonymous, for instance, alcoholism is now classified as a disease. Addictions today, and apparently there is much to be addicted to, are referred to as disease. Of course, a disease is not a moral or sin issue. Disease, it is thought, may stem from a faulty genetic makeup or may be environmental in origin—or some combination thereof. And, I will be happy to admit, there is probably some truth to this notion.

But Jesus did not die on the cross for diseases; He died for our sin. Diseases are treated, so very often with mind and mood altering drugs, and there is a giant industry out there ready to supply the need. A lot of people have a vested interest in turning as many problems as possible into one kind of disease or another. If the preacher is intimidated into adopting the disease paradigm, Jesus becomes some kind of healer and not the Savior. So, there will be pressure to drop the biblical doctrine of sin and adopt the disease model.

A number of well-meaning people have urged me to be more accommodating towards those of other religions and acknowledge that all sincere, loving people are acceptable to God regardless of what they think of or believe about Jesus. The term "relativism" is ordinarily applied to this idea that all religious doctrines are true for the people who believe them. The concept, though often unstated, is—only narrow minded, bigoted people believe Jesus is the only way.

Yes, this "post-modernistic" sentiment is indeed powerful. Some churches function more like social and political agencies rather than gatherings of people who trust in Jesus as Savior and Lord. I have read that some religious leaders are actually advocating dropping the Christian framework, vocabulary, and theology altogether and admitting that they are social workers or political activists and so on. And I applaud this move toward honesty since so many church professionals have abandoned the truth that the primary need for people is reconciliation with God. And pastors in certain denominations will experience pressure upon them to go with the new movements. We must, however, refuse to be intimidated.

At times I have felt intimidated. Preaching a clear and strong gospel message will cause some people to get up and leave right in the middle of the sermon. This has happened to me many times. Sometimes a family member of someone in the church will strongly react to the gospel message and create quite a stir. When it becomes clear that a stand is being taken for the truth of Scripture, it will drive people away who are committed to the idea that all religious teachings are true and equal.

Certain Christian based cults are often lumped in with orthodox, historic Christian churches. I am thinking here of Mormons, Jehovah's Witnesses, Christian Scientists, among others. Since the typical non-believer is either oblivious to or uncaring about the major differences in theology of the cults from mainstream Christianity, they justify the cults on the basis of nothing more substantial than what they gather from the media. And these large and powerful cults work hard at creating a favorable public opinion of themselves. But as a pastor it is part of my job to protect the church by informing people of the difference and the dangers. This gets me into trouble from time to time. Some people perceive of the pastor as a warm, accepting father type, which is fine, but are put off by the pastor who must drive off the wolf and the roaring lion. Here again we must refuse to be intimidated.

Doctrine and theology are not irrelevant. Well, some doctrines are not as critical as others are. My view of the end times is important to me but not critical. My view of the person and work of Jesus, on the other hand, is critical. On the issues of the gospel I can not and will not budge. (The stance we take in defense of the gospel must be humble and gentle, not arrogant or rude.) Paul said that if people come preaching another gospel they must not be tolerated. (see Galatians 1:8) The need and desire to be liked and approved, or the desire to keep your job, must not override our loyalty to Christ and His truth.

In normal times, when there is no great outpouring of the Holy Spirit, few are being converted. Some will be converted through the preaching of the gospel, but it is not like awakening or revival times when many are converted. So there is the temptation to adopt techniques to get people into the pews even if it is not through genuine conversion. Of course I am referring to the church growth movement on the one hand and the false revivals on the other. Excitement, entertainment, and clever marketing skills will bring people into the church, but it results in false conversion, most of the time, and does not represent real growth. In some denominations it is virtually impossible to avoid going with the flow, I admit, but preachers must never lose sight of the fact that faith comes by hearing the preaching of Christ. (see Romans 10:17)

Another dilemma has to do with the need people have to follow and develop their own interests. We are certainly busy people with limited amounts of time especially if there is a home, a family, a job, a school; and the church will just have to take its place in line. When once there were normally two worship services on Sunday, a prayer meeting, a Bible study, choir practice, and other meetings throughout the week, today most of the evangelical Christians make it to the church site or satellite location only once a month. And pastors can be pressured to keep it simple, even close meetings or eliminate some activities entirely.

In some ways I can appreciate the need for personal and family time, but my preference is to have as many ministries and meetings available as possible. We don't want to administrate our programs toward the lowest common denominator, no, as best we can, we want to offer as much as we can.

Pastors will face many forms and sources of intimidation, sometimes from within the church, often from without, even from neighbors. We do not want to be stubborn, unreasonable people who insist on applying the great, old ways, but neither do we want to be intimidated into accepting worldly and unbiblical standards.

☞ Have you any personal experience with sources of intimidation?

☞ Can you describe one such?

☞ How have you dealt with people within the church who have tried to bend you to their will?

# Fifty-seven

# One Last Word on Preaching*

"Light and heat, preaching must have both. Light, the truth of God's word, and heat, the light presented with personal conviction and passion, and in the power of the Holy Spirit."

These words (paraphrased by this author) from Brian Borgman, pastor of Grace Community Church in Gardnerville, Nevada, prompted the inclusion of one last word on preaching.

✢　✢　✢　✢　✢

Charles H. Spurgeon is my favorite preacher. Because of the publication of his many sermons he still speaks and one of his most dramatic declarations is: "I set myself on fire and people come to watch me burn." (I recommend Spurgeon's *Lectures to My Students*, Pilgrim Publications, Pasadena, Texas, Pilgrimpub@aol.com.).

Spurgeon's preaching had both light, the truth of the Word of God, and heat, fueled by his deep concern that the unconverted would come to Jesus and that the saints would glorify and honor God. He preached with compassion and passion at once. (Spurgeon was also a bit of a comedian and would be criticized that he was overly humorous in the pulpit.)

With such preaching there will be little need for entertainment to attract crowds—the gospel message preached with power is compelling enough. There will be no need for techniques and gimmicks when the Word of God is declared by a pastor who has been in communion with Jesus Christ and filled with the Holy Spirit.

The pastor must, additionally, teach the congregation their role in preaching. No preacher can survive without the prayers and support of the congregation. The church must arrive on Sunday morning ready to hear the Word of God, and must expect that the Holy Spirit will speak to them. Therefore a wise pastor will teach the church to be strong in faith and prayer when they arrive for worship. This is illustrated by a quote from Spurgeon. A reporter once asked him, "To what do you attribute your success." Spurgeon replied, "My people pray for me." In fact, a large group gathered every Monday evening to pray for their pastor. There it is. The pastor and the church together, praying and preaching, bringing glory to God.

☞ Do you like to preach?

☞ Would you like to preach?

☞ Have you got a sermon full of light that you set on fire?

*I highly recommend *Preaching and Preachers*, by D. Martin Lloyd-Jones, published by Zondervan Publishing House in 1972. It is available through Amazon.com.

# Appendix

Appendix A, Jonathan Dickinson's sermon *Theology of New Birth,* and Appendix B, C. H. Spurgeon's sermon, *Compel Them To Come In,* can be attached to an email. Use kentphilpott@home.com or go into Earthen Vessel's website, earthenvessel.net and print them out directly from the site. If the appendix is requested by email, it can be zipped or not, and the format is Windows 95.

For a list of sermons on tape by the author visit earthenvessel.net or w3church.org.

# Postscript

After reading a book on preaching I became so discouraged with my own that I thought about giving it up altogether. Then I attended a lecture series on pastoral ministry and at the end I was convinced I ought to leave the ministry.

I hope this book will be an encouragement to preachers and pastors. But, I realize the danger in such a book as this. Herein is compacted decades of experience, and being and doing it all may seem daunting at minimum. The subjects discussed in this book did not come to me suddenly nor do I meet the ideals expressed here either. Preaching and pastoring are learned day by day, month by month, decade by decade. It never ends. And, I am never "there". I am not taking back anything I've written though; it seems to me to be useful material, containing ideas and thoughts worth considering.

If we are called to preach and to pastor, then God Himself will enable us to do His work. It is as straightforward as that. I can trust that He will do it. I may not ever be what I think I ought to be, but I am satisfied that I am becoming who God wants me to be.

# TWO OTHER BOOKS FROM KENT PHILPOTT

*Are You Really Born Again?* and *Why I Am A Christian*
available through Amazon.com

Both books are published by Evangelical Press of
Great Britain. The first book, published in 1998, deals
with understanding true and false conversion. The
second, due out July 2001, is composed of 19 essays
and is suitable for evangelistic purposes.